I0773709

Table Of Contents

The President's Past: Truth, Lies, and the American Dream

Dedication

To the tireless pursuit of truth and justice, even in the face of overwhelming power and political pressure. This book is dedicated to the unwavering commitment of investigative journalists, legal scholars, and citizens who demand accountability from those in positions of authority. It is also dedicated to the memory of those whose voices have been silenced, whose stories have been ignored, and whose struggles for justice have often gone unnoticed. Their courage and perseverance inspire us to seek a more just and equitable society, one where truth prevails and the rule of law is upheld, regardless of political affiliations or personal ambitions. This work is a testament to the enduring importance of independent investigation and the vital role of a free press in holding the powerful accountable.

May this investigation serve as a reminder that no one, regardless of their station, is above the law and that the pursuit of justice is a continuous, collective endeavor. It is a journey that demands our constant vigilance and unwavering dedication to the principles of fairness and equality under the law. The pursuit of justice is a marathon, not a sprint. This dedication reflects our enduring commitment to this race, and our hope that this book contributes to a more informed and engaged citizenry.

Introduction

The life and career of any future president is a subject of intense public scrutiny, but when accusations of criminal activity emerge, the level of scrutiny intensifies exponentially. This book navigates the turbulent waters of such an examination, focusing on the allegations surrounding a future president of the United States. It's a journey into the intricate intersection of law, politics, and public perception, a landscape often obscured by partisan biases and the noise of the 24-hour news cycle. We delve into the specifics of the accusations, meticulously tracing their timeline and examining the evidence presented against the future president. The analysis extends beyond a simple recounting of events; it dissects the legal proceedings, assessing the strength of the evidence, the fairness of the process, and the application of relevant statutes and legal precedents.

We explore the intricacies of forensic accounting, witness testimony, and the challenges of proving criminal intent. Moreover, this work places these legal battles within their broader political context. We analyze the impact of the accusations on public opinion, examining the role of media coverage, political polarization, and the president's approval ratings. We consider the potential consequences of these allegations for the president's legitimacy and the wider political landscape. This book is not merely a chronicle of events; it is an analysis of the systems and processes that shape our understanding of truth and justice in the face of political power. Through careful examination of the facts, a balanced presentation of perspectives, and a commitment to evidence-based reasoning, we aim to illuminate this critical juncture in American history, allowing readers to draw their own informed conclusions. Ultimately, the aim is to encourage critical thinking and informed civic engagement.

Chronology of Allegations

Chapter One

The unfolding of accusations against the president began subtly, almost imperceptibly, a low hum of discontent rising from various corners of the political landscape. The initial whispers, easily dismissed as partisan attacks, centered around inconsistencies in his financial disclosures filed during his gubernatorial campaign. These early allegations, dating back to 2016, involved discrepancies in reported income and asset values, prompting inquiries from state ethics commissions but ultimately yielding no formal charges. The reports, largely buried within local news outlets and quickly overshadowed by the national election cycle, documented vague claims of underreporting income from speaking engagements and potential conflicts of interest related to real estate dealings. Lacking concrete evidence and facing a barrage of counter-arguments and denials, these early probes fizzled out, leaving a lingering sense of unease for some but failing to gain significant traction with the wider electorate.

The narrative shifted significantly in 2018 with the publication of an investigative report by the New York Times. This report, meticulously detailing years of financial transactions, unearthed evidence suggesting potential tax evasion and undisclosed foreign investments. The Times article, citing leaked internal documents and anonymous sources within the president's former accounting firm, painted a picture of a complex web of shell corporations and offshore accounts, raising serious questions about the president's financial transparency and compliance with tax laws. The specific allegations included claims of using shell corporations to conceal income from various sources, including campaign contributions disguised as business transactions, and utilizing offshore accounts to avoid paying taxes on substantial foreign earnings. The timing of the publication, just months before midterm elections, immediately thrust the matter into the heart of the political debate.

The immediate fallout from the New York Times investigation was intense. While the president and his campaign vehemently denied all allegations, claiming the report was a politically motivated "witch hunt," the impact was undeniable. Public opinion polls showed a significant drop in approval ratings, and the opposition party seized the opportunity to launch a renewed push for investigations. The House Oversight Committee launched its own investigation, requesting access to relevant financial documents and summoning key individuals associated with the president's financial affairs to testify. The president's legal team actively fought these requests, arguing against the committee's authority and challenging the relevance of the documents sought. The ensuing legal battles became a protracted and highly publicized affair, further fueling public speculation and deepening the political divide.

Simultaneously, a separate line of inquiry emerged, focusing on allegations of abuse of power. This strand of accusations stemmed from allegations of using his position to enrich himself and his family, including claims of favoritism in awarding lucrative government contracts to companies with ties to his family members. Several whistleblowers came forward, providing evidence of preferential treatment and bypassing standard procurement procedures. One such whistleblower, a former government employee, testified before a Senate committee, alleging direct pressure from the president's office to award a major infrastructure contract to a construction company with known ties to the president's son-in-law. The testimony, while generating considerable media attention, proved difficult to verify independently, and the relevant government agencies found no concrete evidence of wrongdoing after a lengthy internal investigation.

In 2019, further allegations surfaced involving potential obstruction of justice. These accusations stemmed from the president's attempts to interfere with several ongoing investigations into his financial affairs and alleged abuse of power. The claims involved allegations of attempting to influence witness testimony, destroying evidence, and pressuring law enforcement officials to drop or delay investigations. These assertions were largely based on the testimony of several former aides, who described a pattern of intimidation and attempts to manipulate the legal process. The credibility of these witnesses, many of whom had already admitted to committing perjury in other contexts, became a major point of contention during subsequent hearings and legal proceedings.

The year 2020 saw a marked escalation of the legal proceedings, with several key subpoenas being issued and court battles over the president's compliance intensifying. While several attempts were made by the president's legal team to dismiss the cases citing various procedural flaws and lack of evidence, the courts generally ruled against these motions. The accumulation of these legal setbacks, coupled with the continued drip-feed of damaging leaks and media reports, considerably impacted the president's standing with the public. The investigations were still ongoing as of the end of 2020, with no definitive resolution in sight. Meanwhile, the ongoing COVID-

19 pandemic served to overshadow many of the legal developments, causing the media and public focus to temporarily shift to a more pressing health crisis.

The beginning of 2021 marked a new chapter in the unfolding drama. A high-profile legal expert, known for their meticulous approach and independent stance, was called to testify before a special Senate Committee. This expert, having studied the available evidence for months, concluded that while certain actions of the president appeared suspicious, there wasn't enough hard evidence to definitively prove the president engaged in criminal activity. The committee concluded that, while the allegations raised serious ethical questions and gave the appearance of impropriety, there was insufficient evidence to meet the high standard of proof needed for criminal charges. This assessment, though not universally accepted, had a discernible impact on public perception. Despite the lack of criminal charges, the cloud of suspicion continued to linger, especially as further details emerged, including a deeper analysis of specific financial transactions and further witness accounts.

Throughout 2022 and 2023, the ongoing investigations yielded additional information, some of which further strengthened the existing accusations, while other aspects failed to yield definitive conclusions. A renewed focus shifted towards analyzing the potential political implications of the allegations, regardless of their legal outcome. The questions became less about the specifics of the legal processes and more about the damage done to the political system, the erosion of public trust, and the long-term effects on democratic institutions. The investigations eventually concluded without resulting in any criminal charges, but the narrative surrounding the allegations, and their impact on the political discourse, continued to play a central role in the ongoing dialogue about the president's legacy. The lack of conclusive legal action, however, did not equate to the dismissal of the ethical questions raised. Many believe that even without formal criminal charges, the allegations have indelibly shaped public perception of the president and his administration.

The timeline presented here is necessarily incomplete and subject to further developments. New information may emerge that requires a reassessment of existing evidence and interpretations. The objective is to provide a clear and comprehensive account of the allegations, allowing readers to form their own informed opinions based on the available evidence. This meticulously documented timeline serves as the foundation for a more in-depth analysis, exploring the complex intersection of law, politics, and public opinion surrounding these extraordinary accusations. The task ahead involves not only examining the legal intricacies of each allegation, but also understanding their broader implications for American governance and the public's faith in its institutions. The analysis will delve into the nuances of evidence, the credibility of sources, the legal processes, and the political context in which these events unfolded. The goal is to illuminate the often murky waters of political accusations, ensuring a comprehensive and transparent understanding of the multifaceted issues at play.

Categorizing the Charges

The accusations against the president, while seemingly disparate at first glance, can be categorized into several distinct legal areas, facilitating a clearer understanding of their potential implications. This categorization is not intended to pre-judge the merits of each accusation but rather to provide a structured framework for analysis. The lines between these categories can sometimes blur, with individual actions potentially falling under multiple classifications. This inherent complexity underscores the need for careful examination of each allegation within its specific legal context.

The most prominent category centers around alleged financial crimes. These accusations, spanning several years, involve a wide range of potential offenses, each requiring separate legal scrutiny. Allegations of tax evasion, a serious felony, are particularly prominent. These involve claims of underreporting income from various sources, including speaking engagements, real estate transactions, and potential undisclosed investments. The complexity arises not only from the sheer volume of financial transactions involved but also from the intricate web of shell corporations and offshore accounts allegedly used to obscure the president's true financial holdings. Proving tax evasion necessitates demonstrating intent to defraud the government, a significant hurdle for prosecutors. The legal challenge lies in meticulously tracing the flow of funds, demonstrating the president's knowledge of the alleged underreporting, and establishing the necessary mens rea – the guilty mind – required for a conviction. Detailed forensic accounting, expert testimony on financial transactions, and meticulous examination of relevant documents will be crucial in determining the validity of these accusations.

Further allegations within the financial crimes category include potential violations of campaign finance laws. These claims revolve around the financing of his presidential and gubernatorial campaigns, focusing on the origins of substantial donations and potential attempts to circumvent campaign contribution limits. Evidence suggesting "dark money" contributions – donations from undisclosed sources – raises significant legal concerns. Investigating these allegations requires tracing the flow of funds, identifying the true donors, and establishing a connection between the donations and any potential quid pro quo arrangements. The opacity of campaign finance regulations, combined with the inherent difficulty in proving intent, adds considerable complexity to these investigations. Determining whether these allegations constitute criminal violations requires rigorous scrutiny of campaign finance reports, bank records, and communications related to donations.

Beyond financial crimes, a significant portion of the accusations fall under the umbrella of abuse of power. These allegations paint a picture of a president leveraging his office for personal gain and political advantage, potentially violating various federal laws designed to protect the integrity of government. One key area of concern involves alleged obstruction of justice. Accusations include attempts to interfere with ongoing investigations, including attempts to influence witness testimony and suppress evidence. Establishing obstruction of justice typically requires demonstrating an intent to obstruct the course of justice, making it a challenging charge to prove. The evidence needs to show not simply an act that could hinder an investigation, but also a specific intent behind the action. This frequently relies on circumstantial evidence and inferences drawn from the president's actions and statements.

Another dimension of the abuse of power accusations involves allegations of bribery and extortion. These claims suggest that the president used his official position to secure personal benefits, including financial gain and political favors. This could involve leveraging his authority to influence regulatory decisions, awarding lucrative contracts to politically connected individuals, or seeking personal enrichment through official actions. Proving bribery or extortion necessitates establishing a direct link between official actions and the receipt of a benefit. This requires substantial evidence, including communications, financial records, and witness testimony, to demonstrate a clear quid pro quo exchange. The high burden of proof and the potential for conflicting interpretations of actions make these charges exceptionally difficult to prosecute.

A third category centers on potential violations of ethics regulations. While not criminal offenses in the same way as the charges described above, violations of ethics rules can lead to significant political and reputational consequences. These alleged infractions involve potential conflicts of interest, self-dealing, and misuse of public resources for personal gain. While not all ethical lapses rise to the level of criminal activity, they can erode public trust and damage the credibility of the office. Investigations into such allegations often focus on the president's financial disclosures, public statements, and use of government resources. The line between ethically questionable behavior and outright criminal activity can be fine, demanding careful consideration of the context and intent behind actions.

The sheer volume and complexity of the allegations necessitate a multi-faceted approach to analysis. Simply categorizing the charges is only the first step. Each allegation needs to be examined thoroughly, considering the specific legal elements required for a conviction, the available evidence, and the potential defenses that could be raised. The timeline presented earlier provides a chronological overview, but a comprehensive analysis requires delving into the specific legal arguments and precedents relevant to each charge. Furthermore, the political context in which these accusations arose must be considered. The influence of partisan politics, media coverage, and public opinion on the investigation and prosecution of these cases cannot be overlooked. The interaction between legal proceedings and the political landscape presents a significant challenge to any attempt to arrive at an unbiased assessment.

Ultimately, understanding these accusations requires not only a deep dive into the legal intricacies but also a critical examination of the source of the accusations themselves. Were these accusations driven by legitimate concerns about criminal behavior, or are they part of a broader political strategy to undermine the president's legitimacy? This question requires an unbiased evaluation of the credibility of sources, the evidence presented, and the overall political climate. The evidence itself, its interpretation, and the process by which it is evaluated will all be subject to intense scrutiny and debate. The subsequent chapters will explore each category of accusations in greater detail, examining the evidence, legal arguments, and potential outcomes, offering the reader a comprehensive and balanced perspective to reach their own informed conclusions. The goal is not to offer definitive judgments but to provide the tools necessary for informed engagement with this complex and consequential case.

Initial Public Reactions and Media Coverage

The initial public reaction to the allegations against the future president was a complex and rapidly evolving phenomenon, shaped by a confluence of factors including the nature of the accusations themselves, the political climate, and the inherent biases within the media landscape. The accusations, ranging from alleged financial improprieties to potential abuses of power, were met with a spectrum of responses, from outright denial and staunch support to expressions of deep concern and demands for thorough investigations.

The first wave of reporting, largely dominated by cable news networks and online media, was characterized by a frantic pace and a significant degree of sensationalism. Headline after headline screamed of potential scandals, often employing inflammatory language and emphasizing the most dramatic aspects of the allegations. This immediate, unfiltered dissemination of information, before thorough vetting and verification, contributed significantly to the initial public perception, setting a tone that would prove difficult to shift in the subsequent weeks and months. The speed of the news cycle, fueled by social media's instantaneous reach, created an echo chamber effect, reinforcing and amplifying certain narratives while potentially silencing dissenting voices. Analysis during this period often lacked nuance, presenting a simplified binary of "guilty" or "innocent," neglecting the complexities of the legal process and the burden of proof.

Different news outlets exhibited varying degrees of bias, reflecting existing political alignments. Right-leaning media outlets tended to downplay or dismiss the accusations, portraying them as politically motivated attacks designed to sabotage the president's career. They emphasized the president's past achievements and framed the allegations as part of a "witch hunt," employing rhetoric that appealed to their target audience's pre-existing beliefs. Conversely, left-leaning outlets generally reported on the allegations with greater seriousness, stressing the potential gravity of the accusations and calling for transparent investigations. The different framing and emphasis used by these outlets shaped how their respective audiences interpreted the information, reinforcing existing political divisions and contributing to an increasingly polarized climate.

The role of social media in shaping public perception cannot be overstated. Platforms like Twitter and Facebook became battlegrounds for competing narratives, with individuals and organizations disseminating information, often unverified, at an unprecedented rate. The spread of misinformation and disinformation was rampant, further complicating the task of discerning truth from falsehood. The algorithms that govern these platforms tended to prioritize emotionally charged content, leading to the amplification of extreme viewpoints and the marginalization of more moderate perspectives. This created a highly volatile environment, where public opinion was susceptible to manipulation and rapid shifts, making it challenging to accurately assess the true weight of public sentiment.

Independent news organizations and investigative journalism outlets played a crucial role in attempting to provide more balanced and in-depth coverage. These sources, often facing resource constraints and intense pressure, sought to verify information, explore multiple perspectives, and present a more nuanced account of the allegations. Their reporting frequently unearthed crucial details, providing contextual information that was often missing from the initial wave of reporting. However, even these organizations faced challenges in navigating the complexities of the legal process and the intense political pressure surrounding the case. The sheer volume of information, coupled with the inherent difficulty of verifying all claims, made their task exceptionally demanding.

The initial legal responses also played a significant role in shaping public perception. The president's legal team, adopting a strategy of aggressive denial and counter-accusations, further fueled the firestorm of controversy. Their public statements, often delivered through press conferences and carefully crafted media appearances, were meticulously designed to influence public opinion, emphasizing aspects that could potentially garner support while downplaying potentially damaging information. The legal strategies employed, such as delays in providing information or challenging the legitimacy of investigative bodies, became subjects of intense scrutiny and debate, further dividing public opinion.

Public opinion polls conducted during this initial period revealed a sharply divided populace. Support for the president among his base remained strong, with many attributing the allegations to partisan attacks. However, a significant segment of the population expressed serious concerns, demanding transparency and a thorough investigation. The polls also highlighted the significant impact of media consumption on public opinion, with individuals who primarily consumed information from specific news sources exhibiting significantly different levels of support for the president. This divergence further underscored the power of media framing and the challenge of creating a shared understanding of the facts in an increasingly fragmented information environment.

Beyond the immediate media coverage, the initial reaction also saw an outpouring of public commentary from various stakeholders, including political figures, legal experts, and commentators from civil society organizations. These voices often provided contrasting interpretations of the allegations, further amplifying the existing divisions within society. Some individuals and groups actively sought to defend the president, while others called for his immediate resignation or impeachment. The intensity of these public debates underscored the profound political implications of the case, extending beyond the immediate legal context to have far-reaching consequences for the country's political landscape.

The initial days and weeks following the release of the allegations were a period of intense media scrutiny and public debate. The lack of readily available facts and conflicting narratives created a fertile ground for speculation and misinformation. The intense polarization and the fragmented nature of the information ecosystem made it difficult for individuals to form accurate and objective judgements. The speed and scale of the information flow overwhelmed traditional fact-checking mechanisms, making it difficult for many to filter and assess the information they encountered. The lasting impact of this initial period would continue to shape the trajectory of the allegations throughout the entire legal and political process. This highly charged atmosphere would set the stage for a long and drawn-out struggle to determine the truth, a struggle that would test the resilience of democratic institutions and the ability of the public to navigate a complex and often misleading information environment. The analysis of this period serves as a crucial step in understanding the unfolding narrative of the allegations, providing a crucial framework for evaluating the subsequent stages of the unfolding saga. The subsequent chapters will continue to examine the evolution of this complex situation, tracing the ebb and flow of public opinion in relation to the evidence presented and the strategic maneuvering of the various actors involved.

Key Players and Their Roles

The initial firestorm of allegations surrounding the future president's past quickly coalesced around a core group of individuals whose actions and testimonies would shape the narrative for years to come. Understanding their roles and the intricate web of relationships that connected them is crucial to deciphering the complex tapestry of accusations and counter-accusations that followed.

Central to the unfolding drama were the individuals who made the initial accusations. Their motivations, backgrounds, and credibility became immediate points of contention. Were they driven by genuine concerns about wrongdoing, or were other agendas at play – personal vendettas, political ambitions, or financial gain? Scrutinizing their pasts, examining their relationships with the president, and analyzing the consistency and corroboration of their claims became paramount in assessing the validity of the accusations. The thoroughness of their accounts, the specifics provided, and the presence or absence of independent verification were all crucial elements in the ensuing investigation. One notable accuser, a former business associate, presented detailed financial records allegedly demonstrating illicit transactions and fraudulent activities. Their testimony, bolstered by supporting documentation, gained immediate traction, while others, offering more anecdotal evidence, faced greater skepticism. The initial wave of accusations also included whistleblowers from within the president's inner circle, each with a unique perspective and level of access to potentially incriminating information. These individuals, often operating under the cloak of anonymity, added layers of complexity to the narrative, highlighting the potential for both internal dissent and a network of complicity. The credibility of their accounts often hinged on the ability to independently verify their claims and establish their motivation for coming forward, thus demanding a meticulous investigation into their backgrounds and potential biases.

The investigative journalists who first reported on these allegations played a critical role in shaping public perception. Their ability to gather, verify, and present information to the public was constantly scrutinized, particularly in the context of a highly polarized political climate. Their reputations, their sources, and their methodology all became subjects of intense debate and scrutiny. Some journalists were accused of bias, while others were praised for their rigorous fact-checking and dedication to journalistic integrity. Their choices in focusing on certain aspects of the story while minimizing or ignoring others were also subject to considerable analysis and critique, highlighting the potential for subtle biases to shape the unfolding narrative. The media landscape itself, characterized by its fragmentation and the proliferation of partisan outlets, served to exacerbate the challenge of separating fact from opinion, further complicating the task of forming an accurate understanding of the situation. The influence of social media, characterized by its speed and virality, further blurred the lines between credible reporting and outright disinformation, posing significant challenges to the public's ability to navigate the deluge of information.

The legal professionals involved – the lawyers representing the president and the prosecutors investigating the allegations – played crucial roles in defining the legal framework surrounding the accusations and guiding the trajectory of the legal proceedings. The skill, experience, and strategic choices of these lawyers profoundly influenced the course of the investigations and trials. The tactics employed by each side, from the aggressive cross-examination of witnesses to the careful selection of evidence presented, became key elements in the evolving narrative. The legal battles were often characterized by protracted negotiations, appeals, and court decisions that added new layers of complexity and uncertainty to the situation. The judges overseeing these proceedings played an equally pivotal role, their impartiality and fairness directly affecting the perception of justice and the ultimate outcome of the legal battles. Their rulings on evidence admissibility, procedural matters, and the overall conduct of the case were crucial in shaping public opinion and influencing the perceptions of fairness and transparency in the legal process. The scrutiny placed on these judicial actors, on the integrity of their decisions, and the potential for conflicts of interest also added further complexity to the overarching narrative.

Beyond the immediate players, various government agencies and oversight bodies also played a significant role in investigating the allegations. The investigations undertaken by these agencies, their conclusions, and the transparency of their findings all became subjects of intense public scrutiny and debate.

The resources, expertise, and independence of these government entities became key determinants in the public's assessment of the credibility and fairness of the investigation. The timelines for the investigations, the choice of investigative techniques, and the eventual dissemination of findings were all subjected to careful analysis and criticism. Differences in conclusions or approaches between different agencies often fueled additional controversy and debate, adding layers of complexity to an already intricate situation. External pressure, political maneuvering, and the sheer weight of public opinion all influenced the course of these official investigations.

The eventual impact on the president's career, his public image, and the broader political landscape cannot be overstated. The allegations, irrespective of their ultimate legal outcome, profoundly influenced the way the president was perceived by the public and his ability to govern. The public's response, constantly shifting based on the flow of information and the unfolding legal battles, demonstrated the dynamic interplay between law, politics, and public opinion. The president's supporters remained steadfast in their belief in his innocence, often highlighting his positive contributions and questioning the motivations of his detractors. Conversely, his critics expressed deep concern about the allegations, questioning his suitability for office and demanding full accountability. Analyzing the shifts in public opinion, the influence of media narratives, and the strategic communications of different political actors is essential to fully grasp the impact of this protracted saga on the broader political discourse. The lasting effects on the nation's political landscape, the polarization of public opinion, and the evolving trust in institutions remain profound and far-reaching consequences of the intertwined legal and political battles. The analysis of these long-term consequences is essential to understanding the complex interplay between law, politics, and the erosion or reinforcement of public trust in democratic systems.

Legal Framework and Relevant Statutes

The accusations leveled against the future president, ranging from financial impropriety to potential abuses of power, necessitate a careful examination of the relevant legal framework. Understanding the statutes and precedents governing these alleged offenses is crucial to assessing the merits of the claims and determining whether the actions in question actually constitute criminal violations under U.S. law. This analysis avoids offering legal conclusions, instead focusing on providing the reader with the necessary context to understand the legal complexities involved. The accusations span multiple jurisdictions and legal domains, demanding a multifaceted legal analysis that considers both federal and state laws.

One significant area of focus involves potential violations of campaign finance laws. The Federal Election Campaign Act (FECA) and related regulations govern the disclosure of contributions and expenditures during political campaigns. Allegations of undisclosed or illegally sourced donations, the use of "dark money" through shell corporations or non-profit organizations, and the exceeding of contribution limits all fall under the purview of FECA. The penalties for violating FECA can be substantial, including civil fines, criminal prosecution, and even disqualification from holding office. Interpretations of FECA have evolved over time, particularly regarding the definition of "contribution" and the complexities surrounding independent expenditures. Supreme Court cases such as Citizens United v. FEC and McCain-Feingold significantly shaped the legal landscape concerning campaign finance, raising crucial questions about the balance between free speech and campaign finance regulation. Furthermore, state-level campaign finance laws vary, potentially leading to a patchwork of legal standards and interpretations across different jurisdictions. Analyzing the specific allegations through the prism of both federal and relevant state laws is paramount to a comprehensive understanding of the legal issues at hand.

Beyond campaign finance, the allegations encompass possible violations of tax laws. The Internal Revenue

Code (IRC) is a vast and intricate body of law governing taxation in the United States. Allegations of tax evasion, including underreporting income, claiming false deductions, or engaging in offshore tax haven schemes, are serious offenses with severe consequences. The burden of proof lies with the prosecution to demonstrate beyond a reasonable doubt that the taxpayer knowingly and willfully attempted to evade taxes. Proving intent is often a key battleground in such cases, relying on circumstantial evidence such as unusual banking transactions, complex financial structures, and inconsistencies between financial records and tax returns. Case law concerning tax evasion demonstrates the courts' careful scrutiny of evidence to ensure that the conviction is not based on mere negligence or unintentional errors, but on a deliberate attempt to defraud the government. Understanding the nuances of tax law and the legal precedents concerning tax evasion is necessary for interpreting the allegations fairly.

Potential violations of federal lobbying laws represent another critical aspect of the legal investigation. The Honest Leadership and Open Government Act (HLOGA) and other related statutes regulate lobbying activities aimed at influencing government officials. Allegations of unreported lobbying efforts, exceeding lobbying expenditure limits, or using improper influence tactics require examination under these statutes. The act defines lobbying extensively and mandates strict reporting requirements. Proving violations under HLOGA often necessitates investigating the nature of communication between lobbyists and government officials, determining whether the communication aimed at influencing legislative action, and establishing whether the proper disclosure requirements were met. Judicial interpretations of HLOGA have clarified the definition of "lobbying" in various contexts and clarified the threshold for criminal prosecution.

The allegations also touch upon potential violations of conflict-of-interest rules. These rules vary depending on the level of government involved, and their interpretation is often complex and context-specific. These regulations aim to prevent officials from using their positions for personal gain or the benefit of private entities. The accusations involve an examination of the line between personal enrichment and legitimate business activities, with the key question being whether the actions constituted an abuse of power or a misuse of official position for personal or financial advantage. Case law surrounding conflict of interest provides a useful precedent for examining the allegations, highlighting instances where courts have found violations based on the appearance of impropriety even if there was no direct evidence of illicit intent.

Furthermore, the potential for obstruction of justice must be considered. This crime involves acts that impede or obstruct the lawful functions of law enforcement or judicial investigations. Allegations of destroying evidence, intimidating witnesses, or making false statements to law enforcement are all potentially serious offenses. Establishing the intent to obstruct justice is a key component of proving this crime, and the burden of proof rests on the prosecution to demonstrate the defendant acted with knowledge of the illegality of their actions and with the purpose of impeding an investigation. Case law on obstruction of justice reveals a rigorous legal standard, requiring a clear link between the alleged actions and the intention to hamper a legitimate investigation.

The complexities of the legal framework underscore the necessity for a nuanced analysis. Many of the statutes involved have intricate requirements and often involve ambiguous provisions, leaving room for legal interpretation and debate. The analysis requires not only an understanding of the specific legal provisions but also a thorough consideration of relevant case precedents. This examination demonstrates the need for a careful, fact-based approach, avoiding hasty judgments based on incomplete information or biased narratives. The challenge lies in disentangling complex financial transactions, evaluating the veracity of conflicting testimonies, and determining whether the actions, even if morally questionable, actually meet the legal threshold for criminal offenses. The investigation demands a comprehensive approach, considering the interplay of various legal statutes, examining the relevant case law, and allowing for the possibility of multiple interpretations of the evidence. Ultimately, it is the task of the judicial system to determine guilt or innocence according to the established legal principles and processes, while the role of this book is to provide readers with the tools necessary to understand the complex legal dimensions of the accusations.

Analysis of Financial Records

Chapter Two

This section delves into the meticulous examination of the financial records associated with the allegations against the president. The analysis presented here is not merely a recitation of numbers and transactions; it's a deep dive into the intricate web of financial dealings, aiming to unravel potential irregularities and shed light on the alleged criminal activity. We will scrutinize bank statements, tax returns, campaign finance reports, real estate transactions, and any other relevant financial documents, employing a rigorous, evidence-based approach. Crucially, we will rely heavily on the interpretations and analyses provided by forensic accountants and other financial experts, whose expertise is indispensable in deciphering the complexities of high-level finance.

The first step in our analysis is to establish a clear timeline of relevant financial transactions. This timeline will serve as a foundational roadmap, allowing us to track the flow of funds and identify any potentially suspicious patterns or anomalies. Each transaction will be examined in detail, considering its source, destination, amount, and the stated purpose. Discrepancies between stated purposes and the actual nature of the transaction will be carefully noted and investigated further. We will also consider the context surrounding each transaction, taking into account the prevailing political climate and the president's activities at the time.

For instance, one area of particular interest involves a series of large, undocumented cash deposits made into accounts controlled by the president during a specific period. While the president's legal team has offered explanations for these deposits, we will scrutinize these explanations against the available evidence, including bank records, witness testimonies, and relevant financial regulations. The analysis will encompass a detailed comparison of these explanations with the actual financial records, highlighting any inconsistencies or contradictions. Furthermore, we will explore the possibility of these funds originating from illicit sources, drawing upon established investigative techniques and expert interpretations. This will involve examining the financial profiles of individuals or entities linked to these transactions to ascertain whether these parties have a history of involvement in illegal activities.

Another key aspect of this analysis is the examination of the president's tax returns. Tax returns are a crucial source of information regarding financial activities, as they provide a snapshot of income, deductions, and tax liabilities. Any discrepancies or inconsistencies identified in the president's tax returns will be investigated thoroughly, with particular attention paid to potential instances of tax evasion, underreporting of income, or claiming inappropriate deductions. We will also cross-reference the tax return data with other financial records, such as bank statements and real estate transactions, to verify the accuracy and completeness of the reported information. The expertise of tax law specialists will be vital in this analysis, ensuring that we adhere to all applicable regulations and legal frameworks.

The role of forensic accounting is paramount in this analysis. Forensic accountants possess specialized skills in investigating financial fraud and uncovering hidden transactions. Their expertise allows us to delve into the intricacies of complex financial arrangements, often revealing hidden links and patterns that might otherwise go unnoticed. In this case, forensic accountants were employed to analyze vast quantities of financial data, applying advanced analytical techniques to identify potentially suspicious transactions. Their findings, complete with detailed explanations and supporting documentation, will form a cornerstone of this section. We will thoroughly examine their reports, critically assessing their methodologies and conclusions. Any areas of uncertainty or potential bias will be addressed openly and transparently.

Beyond forensic accounting, expert testimony from other financial professionals will be invaluable. These experts may include financial analysts, economists, and specialists in areas like money laundering and international finance. Their insights will provide crucial context and perspective, enriching our understanding of the financial transactions under scrutiny. For instance, one expert provided crucial insight into a series of overseas transactions that initially appeared innocuous, but after careful analysis, were found to involve shell corporations and complex financial maneuvers designed to obscure the true origins and destination of significant sums of money.

Furthermore, the analysis will include a comprehensive examination of the president's real estate holdings and transactions. This investigation will involve scrutinizing property records, mortgage documents, and sales agreements, searching for any signs of illicit financial activity or attempts to conceal assets. For example, a discrepancy was uncovered between the reported value of a property owned by the president and the actual market value. This discrepancy will be explored in detail, investigating possible reasons for the difference, including the possibility of undervaluing the property to avoid higher tax assessments. All findings will be substantiated with evidence and expert analysis to ensure an accurate and impartial presentation.

This section will also address the legal challenges related to accessing and utilizing this financial data. Obtaining financial records often involves navigating intricate legal procedures, including subpoenas, court orders, and privacy concerns. The process of obtaining and verifying the authenticity of these documents will be documented transparently. Any legal challenges encountered during the investigation, such as arguments regarding the privilege of certain documents or disputes over the interpretation of financial regulations, will be discussed in detail.

Finally, the analysis presented here is not intended to reach a conclusion on the guilt or innocence of the president, but rather to present a comprehensive and unbiased examination of the financial evidence. The aim is to provide readers with the information needed to form their own informed judgments based on a clear and thorough presentation of facts and expert interpretations. This analysis represents a significant undertaking, requiring meticulous attention to detail, rigorous fact-checking, and a commitment to upholding the highest standards of journalistic integrity. The information presented here forms a crucial part of the broader investigation into the allegations facing the president, providing critical context and insight into the complexities of the case. The subsequent chapters will build on this foundation, examining additional evidence and exploring the broader political and legal ramifications of these accusations.

Forensic Accounting and Expert Testimony

The labyrinthine world of high-level finance often requires specialized expertise to navigate. While the previous section laid out the raw data—bank statements, tax returns, property deeds, and campaign finance disclosures—understanding their significance necessitates the lens of forensic accounting. This discipline, often described as financial detective work, goes beyond the simple auditing of accounts. Forensic accountants possess a unique skill set, combining accounting proficiency with investigative techniques. They are trained to identify anomalies, uncover hidden transactions, and trace the flow of funds, often uncovering evidence of fraud, embezzlement, or money laundering that might otherwise remain obscured within the complexities of legitimate financial activities.

In this case, the forensic accountants engaged in the investigation were tasked with a particularly challenging mandate: disentangling years of complex financial transactions involving numerous entities, both domestic and international. Their work involved not just examining individual documents but also piecing together a comprehensive picture of the president's financial network, identifying relationships between seemingly disparate entities, and establishing the provenance of funds. This involved sophisticated techniques like tracing the movement of money through shell corporations, identifying unusual patterns of deposits and withdrawals, and cross-referencing financial records with other forms of evidence, such as travel itineraries and communication records.

One of the key areas of focus was the president's real estate holdings. The investigation uncovered a pattern of unusually favorable loan terms, often secured from lenders with questionable reputations or opaque ownership structures. The forensic accountants meticulously examined these loans, comparing the terms with market rates and searching for any evidence of preferential treatment, bribery, or undue influence. They also scrutinized the valuation of the properties involved, looking for any signs of inflated appraisals or other irregularities that could have artificially inflated the president's net worth or facilitated tax evasion. The analysis extended to the identification of previously undisclosed assets and liabilities, an essential step in establishing a complete and accurate picture of the president's financial status.

The complexities did not end with real estate. The investigation also encompassed the president's campaign finances. Campaign finance laws are notoriously intricate, and violations can be difficult to prove. Forensic accountants played a crucial role in analyzing campaign contributions, expenditures, and fundraising activities, searching for evidence of illegal contributions, undisclosed donors, or improper use of campaign funds. This included scrutinizing the source of donations, identifying potential conflicts of interest, and tracing the flow of funds to determine whether any money was diverted for personal use or other illegitimate purposes. The challenge was amplified by the president's extensive international business dealings, requiring the accountants to navigate varying legal frameworks and accounting standards across different jurisdictions.

Expert testimony is central to the legal process, particularly in complex financial cases. The forensic accountants' findings did not exist in a vacuum; their work culminated in detailed reports and expert testimony presented in various legal proceedings. Their testimony, in essence, translates the intricate world of financial transactions into plain language that can be understood by judges, juries, and the public. This requires not only a deep understanding of financial principles but also the ability to communicate complex technical information in a clear, concise, and persuasive manner. The effectiveness of their testimony hinges on several factors, including their qualifications, their experience, the rigor of their methodology, and the clarity of their presentation. The reliability and credibility of their evidence are key factors that influence the outcome of legal proceedings and public perception.

During their testimony, the forensic accountants were subjected to rigorous cross-examination. Defense attorneys attempted to challenge their methodologies, question their interpretations, and raise doubts about the validity of their findings. This adversarial process is a critical element of the legal system, designed to ensure that all evidence is thoroughly vetted and that only reliable information is considered. The forensic accountants' ability to withstand this scrutiny, to defend their analyses, and to maintain the integrity of their findings under pressure is crucial to their credibility. The cross-examination process itself often reveals inconsistencies or weaknesses in the evidence presented, allowing for a more comprehensive and nuanced understanding of the facts.

A significant aspect of the forensic accountants' work involved the application of advanced data analytics techniques. The sheer volume of financial data involved in this investigation far exceeded the capabilities of traditional manual methods. The accountants utilized specialized software and algorithms to identify patterns, anomalies, and other irregularities that might have gone undetected through manual review. This data-driven approach allowed them to analyze vast quantities of information efficiently, identifying potential leads and connections that would have been impossible to discern through conventional methods. This aspect brought to the fore the increasing reliance on technology in forensic accounting investigations, making the analysis not only more efficient but also more thorough.

The application of these cutting-edge technologies raised its own set of questions regarding data security and privacy. The handling of sensitive financial data requires the strictest adherence to confidentiality and security protocols. Forensic accountants operate within a rigorous legal and ethical framework, ensuring the protection of sensitive information and adhering to all applicable data privacy regulations. The integrity of the data itself, its security from alteration or manipulation, and the chain of custody all played a vital role in the admissibility of the evidence presented.

Furthermore, the forensic accountants' work did not exist in isolation. Their findings were corroborated and contextualized by the contributions of other experts, such as financial analysts, economists, and legal scholars. These experts offered different perspectives and provided a more holistic understanding of the financial activities under scrutiny. The collaborative nature of the investigation underscores the complexities of high-level finance investigations and the need for a multidisciplinary approach.

The analysis of the financial evidence, as conducted by the forensic accountants and presented through expert testimony, formed a critical pillar of the overall investigation. The evidence, meticulously documented and analyzed, allowed for a deeper understanding of the president's financial dealings, providing context and insight into the accusations levied against him. While the findings themselves are complex and require careful analysis, their presentation and interpretation by qualified experts offer a crucial perspective on the allegations, allowing for a more informed assessment of the situation. The following chapters will explore how this forensic accounting evidence interacts with other aspects of the case, ultimately contributing to a broader understanding of the intersection of law, politics, and public perception. The aim remains to present the facts clearly and allow readers to draw their own informed conclusions.

Witness Testimony and Credibility Assessments

The forensic accounting evidence, painstakingly detailed and meticulously analyzed, provided a strong foundation for the investigation, but it was far from the complete picture. To fully understand the allegations against the future president, we needed to consider another crucial element: witness testimony. These accounts, offered under oath and subject to rigorous cross-examination, painted a more human picture of the events, adding layers of context and perspective to the cold, hard numbers presented in financial records. However, witness testimony, while potentially powerful, is also inherently subjective and susceptible to bias. Evaluating its reliability requires a careful and critical analysis, a process that goes far beyond simply accepting statements at face value.

One of the central challenges in assessing witness credibility lies in understanding the inherent limitations of human memory. Our recollections are not perfect recordings of events; rather, they are reconstructions, susceptible to distortion, omission, and embellishment over time. Factors such as stress, trauma, or the passage of years can significantly impact the accuracy of a witness's account. For instance, a witness recalling a meeting that took place years ago might inadvertently conflate details with other similar meetings, creating a composite memory that deviates from the actual event. This phenomenon is well-documented in legal and psychological research, highlighting the need for caution in accepting witness accounts without careful scrutiny.

Furthermore, the inherent biases of witnesses must be considered. Individual beliefs, preconceived notions, personal relationships with involved parties, and even the subtle influence of leading questions during interviews can all color a witness's testimony. A witness who harbors strong political affiliations, for example, might unconsciously interpret ambiguous events in a way that favors their preferred candidate, inadvertently distorting their recollection. Similarly, a witness with a personal vendetta against the accused might subconsciously exaggerate certain details or omit others that contradict their narrative. The potential for conscious or unconscious bias represents a significant challenge in evaluating the reliability of witness accounts.

This is not to suggest that all witnesses' testimony is inherently unreliable. Many witnesses provide honest and accurate accounts, offering valuable insights into the events under investigation. However, it is crucial to employ rigorous methods to assess the credibility of each witness. The legal system employs several techniques to evaluate testimony, including observing the witness's demeanor on the stand, assessing their consistency across different accounts, and analyzing their potential biases. Independent corroboration of the witness's statements through other forms of evidence is equally crucial. The presence of corroborating evidence adds significant weight to a witness's account, enhancing its credibility and mitigating the potential for bias.

In this particular case, we encountered a wide range of witness testimonies, each possessing its own unique challenges and considerations. Some witnesses were individuals with direct knowledge of specific transactions or meetings, offering firsthand accounts of events pertinent to the investigation. Others offered circumstantial evidence, providing context or background information that helped to illuminate the broader picture. For example, several former employees of the president's businesses provided detailed accounts of their interactions with him, shedding light on his management style and his interactions with other key players. Their testimonies, however, needed to be carefully evaluated. Several had personal grievances against the president, leading to the potential for bias. This prompted careful examination of their statements, verifying facts through other sources and comparing their accounts to other available evidence.

Another crucial aspect in the credibility assessment was the examination of witness motivations. Were there any financial incentives, political pressures, or personal vendettas that could have influenced their testimony? The possibility of coercion or intimidation also required careful consideration. For instance, one witness, initially reluctant to testify, later came forward with crucial information after receiving assurances of protection from potential retaliation. Analyzing their motivation and the context in which their testimony emerged became as important as the content of their testimony itself.

Moreover, the consistency of a witness's statements across multiple interviews or depositions is a significant factor in determining their credibility. A witness who provides substantially different accounts of the same events on different occasions raises serious concerns about the accuracy and reliability of their testimony. Discrepancies might indicate an attempt to deceive, a flawed memory, or a simple misunderstanding of events. Careful comparison of the witness's statements, coupled with a detailed examination of any inconsistencies, helps to gauge the overall reliability of their account.

In the case of expert witnesses, the assessment of credibility involves a different set of criteria. While their testimony is informed by specialized knowledge and expertise, it is still subject to scrutiny. The credentials and experience of the expert, the methodology used in reaching their conclusions, and the potential for bias in their analysis all require careful evaluation. The court often examines whether an expert's opinion is grounded in established scientific principles or accepted professional standards, ensuring the testimony is relevant, reliable, and helpful to the trier of fact.

The process of evaluating witness testimony is not an exact science; rather, it requires a careful balancing of several factors. The absence of direct corroboration for a particular account doesn't necessarily invalidate it, and the presence of corroboration doesn't automatically guarantee its accuracy. The overall assessment depends on a careful weighing of all available evidence, considering potential biases, and evaluating the consistency and plausibility of the witness's statements within the broader context of the case.

Ultimately, the role of the investigative journalist, and indeed the role of any responsible consumer of information, is to approach witness testimony with a critical and discerning eye. While human accounts offer invaluable insights, their inherent limitations demand careful evaluation. By analyzing the witness's background, motivations, potential biases, and the consistency of their statements, we can develop a more nuanced understanding of the information provided and arrive at a more informed and balanced conclusion. The weight assigned to each witness's testimony, therefore, depends on a careful, holistic assessment that acknowledges both its potential value and its inherent limitations. Only through such a rigorous approach can we hope to draw meaningful conclusions about the events in question and make an informed judgment about the allegations levied against the future president. The analysis of witness testimony, therefore, remains a critical component in the overall assessment, providing a vital human element to the otherwise dry financial data and legal documents.

Physical Evidence and its Interpretation

The forensic accounting, bolstered by witness testimonies, provided a compelling narrative, but the investigation demanded a deeper dive into the realm of physical evidence. This realm, often portrayed dramatically in crime procedurals, requires meticulous attention to detail and a profound understanding of its inherent limitations. The value of physical evidence lies not just in its existence, but in its proper handling, documentation, and interpretation. A single misplaced document, a contaminated sample, or a flawed analysis can unravel even the most meticulously constructed case.

One of the most crucial aspects of handling physical evidence is maintaining an unbroken chain of custody. This rigorous process ensures that the evidence's integrity remains intact from the moment it's collected until it's presented in court. Every person who handles the evidence, from the initial collecting officer to the expert witness, must be documented. This documentation includes the date and time of acquisition, the location, the individual responsible for its handling, and a detailed description of the evidence itself. Any deviation from this strict protocol can severely compromise the admissibility of the evidence in a legal setting, rendering it useless in a court of law.

In the case of the future president, several pieces of physical evidence emerged during the investigation. These included electronic devices, such as computers and cell phones, which contained emails, text messages, and other digital communications. The retrieval and analysis of this data involved specialized techniques, adhering to strict protocols to ensure the data's authenticity and prevent tampering or accidental corruption. The process involved creating forensic images of the hard drives and memory cards, ensuring that the original data remained untouched. This meticulous approach is essential because the very act of retrieving data can alter its integrity.

The examination of these electronic devices became a significant part of the investigation. Experts were called upon to extract data, analyze patterns of communication, and corroborate or contradict statements given by witnesses. For instance, emails exchanged between the future president and associates could shed light on the nature of their financial dealings, providing crucial context to the financial transactions uncovered through forensic accounting. Text messages, with their often informal and less guarded nature, might offer insights into motivations and intentions, revealing information not explicitly stated in formal documents. However, the interpretation of this digital evidence required careful consideration. Deleted files could be recovered and examined, but the context surrounding their deletion would need to be considered. Were the files deleted routinely, or did the deletion suggest an attempt to conceal incriminating information? The interpretation hinges not just on the content of the data but also on the context of its creation, access, and deletion.

Beyond electronic communications, physical documents also played a crucial role. This could include contracts, invoices, bank statements, and personal correspondence. Each document underwent rigorous examination to determine authenticity and potential alterations. Sophisticated techniques like comparing ink types, analyzing paper fibers, and employing handwriting analysis were utilized to verify the documents' origins and integrity. For example, a seemingly innocuous contract could hide crucial clauses written in incredibly small print, or altered dates, or even forged signatures. These require specialized equipment and expertise to reveal the manipulations. Moreover, the provenance of these documents – how they were obtained, where they were stored, and the chain of custody associated with them – all played a key role in determining their reliability and admissibility. A document found casually tucked away in a desk drawer might be viewed differently than one obtained through a lawfully executed search warrant. The legal admissibility of any piece of physical evidence is intricately linked to its procurement and handling.

Another category of physical evidence included tangible assets like real estate properties or luxury items. The investigation might involve assessing the actual value of these assets, verifying ownership records, and investigating how they were acquired. This analysis would include examining property deeds, comparing declared values to market values, and exploring the paper trail of financial transactions associated with these purchases. Discrepancies between the declared value and the market price could indicate tax evasion, money laundering, or other fraudulent activities. Similarly, the provenance of luxury items, such as expensive jewelry or high-end cars, needed to be investigated. The purchase records, the declared sources of funds, and the overall lifestyle of the individual could be compared to identify inconsistencies and point towards potential wrongdoing.

The interpretation of physical evidence is rarely straightforward. Context is paramount. A single piece of evidence, taken in isolation, might seem innocuous. However, when analyzed alongside other pieces of evidence – financial records, witness testimony, and digital communications – it can take on a new significance, contributing to a broader narrative of potential wrongdoing. For example, a seemingly ordinary receipt could become incriminating when linked to a pattern of suspicious transactions. The investigative process often involves piecing together a complex puzzle, where each piece of physical evidence represents a small fragment of a larger picture.

Expert testimony plays a critical role in the interpretation of physical evidence. Forensic scientists, document examiners, digital forensics specialists, and other experts provide their professional opinions on the evidence, explaining the technical details and offering their interpretations. Their testimony is subject to rigorous cross-examination, where opposing lawyers challenge their findings and attempt to expose any weaknesses in their analysis. The credibility of the experts, their qualifications, and the methodology they employed all become subject to scrutiny. The strength of their conclusions depends not only on the technical soundness of their analysis but also on their ability to clearly and effectively communicate their findings to the court. Consequently, the expert's presentation and their ability to withstand rigorous cross-examination are as critical as the underlying scientific basis of their analysis. The judge and jury then weigh this evidence alongside other factors to determine its impact on the overall case. The absence of definitive conclusions from the physical evidence analysis does not necessarily equate to a lack of value. The lack of a particular piece of evidence may itself be valuable, pointing to a possible attempt at concealment or destruction of evidence. The careful examination and thorough documentation of the absence of particular types of evidence can often support conclusions as effectively as the presence of such evidence. The weight given to physical evidence ultimately depends on the totality of the circumstances, the credibility of the experts, and the overall context of the investigation. It's not just about the evidence itself, but also the story that the evidence tells.

Legal Challenges and Procedural Issues

The forensic analysis and physical evidence, while compelling in certain aspects, presented a significant hurdle: admissibility in a court of law. The legal challenges weren't merely theoretical; they were deeply intertwined with the procedural steps taken during the investigation. The prosecution's case rested not only on the strength of its evidence but also on its ability to navigate the complex landscape of legal procedure. The admissibility of evidence, a cornerstone of any legal proceeding, hinges on a multitude of factors, each capable of derailing even the most meticulously assembled case. The rules of evidence, varying slightly across jurisdictions, are designed to ensure fairness, prevent prejudice, and guarantee the reliability of information presented before a court. These rules dictate what types of evidence are permissible, how they are presented, and the level of scrutiny to which they are subjected.

One significant challenge related to the chain of custody of certain key documents. The prosecution had to demonstrate an unbroken chain of possession from the initial seizure or acquisition of the documents through their handling, storage, and presentation in court. Any gaps or inconsistencies in this chain could raise serious doubts about the authenticity and integrity of the evidence, potentially leading to its exclusion from the trial. This was particularly crucial in the case of digital documents, where the possibility of alteration or tampering is significantly higher than with physical paper documents. Sophisticated digital forensics experts were needed to rigorously verify the integrity of the digital files, accounting for every access, modification, and transfer, a task that proved both complex and time-consuming. The defense team, naturally, was intensely scrutinizing these procedures, looking for any opportunity to challenge the admissibility of the evidence on the grounds of compromised chain of custody.

Beyond the chain of custody, the question of relevance also played a critical role. The prosecution needed to demonstrate that each piece of evidence was directly relevant to the charges against the future president. Irrelevant evidence, even if authentic, could be excluded to avoid confusing the jury or unduly influencing their judgment. This often involved nuanced legal arguments, requiring the prosecution to meticulously connect the evidence to specific alleged offenses. The line between relevant and irrelevant is not always clear-cut, and the defense would be expected to vigorously challenge any evidence deemed remotely tenuous or potentially prejudicial. For example, a series of emails discussing unrelated political strategies, if somehow linked to a financial transaction under scrutiny, might face intense scrutiny regarding relevance and potential for undue prejudice. The judge, acting as a gatekeeper, would have the ultimate authority to decide on the admissibility of each piece of evidence based on its perceived relevance and probative value versus its potential to mislead or prejudice the jury.

The issue of hearsay also loomed large. Hearsay, essentially secondhand evidence, is generally inadmissible unless it falls under specific exceptions. Many of the allegations relied on accounts from individuals who had not directly witnessed the alleged criminal activity but had heard about it from others. Establishing the credibility of such testimony, and demonstrating its exception from the hearsay rule, was an uphill battle. The prosecution would have to carefully demonstrate that the sources of such information were reliable and that the information relayed accurately reflected the actual events. Furthermore, the defense could be expected to vigorously challenge the reliability of hearsay evidence, exploring the possibility of misinterpretations, exaggerations, or deliberate fabrications. The reliability of witnesses, their motives, and the potential for bias would come under intense scrutiny. The defense would likely argue that such hearsay evidence lacked sufficient probative value and could potentially unfairly prejudice the jury against the defendant.

Procedural issues further complicated the picture. Timing was crucial. Delays in the investigation, or procedural missteps, could trigger legal challenges based on violations of the defendant's rights under the law. The prosecution had to carefully balance the need for thorough investigation with the requirement of timely proceedings, ensuring that the defendant's right to a speedy trial wasn't violated. Any perceived irregularities, such as unreasonable delays in obtaining search warrants or presenting evidence, could be grounds for dismissal or significant limitations on the use of evidence gathered. This was especially true concerning the potential use of wiretaps and other forms of electronic surveillance, which are subject to stringent legal requirements.

The question of due process was paramount. The legal system is structured to ensure a fair trial, encompassing the defendant's right to counsel, access to evidence, the ability to cross-examine witnesses, and to present a defense. Any perceived infringement of these rights would likely be challenged, potentially leading to the exclusion of evidence or even the dismissal of charges. The defense team would aggressively scrutinize every step of the investigation and the prosecution's approach, searching for any potential procedural errors that might invalidate the case. This would include examining whether the defendant's rights were fully respected during interrogations, searches, and seizures. In short, even minor procedural glitches could have cascading effects, compromising the credibility of the entire prosecution's case.

Moreover, the admissibility of expert testimony added another layer of complexity. The prosecution relied heavily on expert witnesses to interpret complex data and explain technical details to the jury. However, the admissibility of this testimony was contingent upon the qualifications of the experts, their methodologies, and the reliability of their findings. The defense could challenge the qualifications of an expert witness, the validity of their methods, or the basis of their conclusions. They could introduce their own expert witnesses to offer counterarguments, potentially creating a battle of experts, each side presenting its own version of the evidence's interpretation. This would not simply be a contest of scientific facts; it would also involve a deep dive into the professional credentials and reputations of each expert witness. The jury would then have to evaluate the credibility of conflicting expert opinions, which is a task requiring careful consideration and a level of critical thinking often beyond the everyday experience of the average person.

Furthermore, the political context of the case added to the inherent complexity. While the legal arguments would center on the admissible evidence and procedural fairness, the underlying political climate would inevitably influence public perception and could impact the jurors' impartiality. The media's portrayal of the case, the statements made by political figures, and the prevailing public sentiment could all play a significant, albeit indirect, role in shaping the outcome. This political context would necessitate a cautious approach for both sides, ensuring the avoidance of any actions that might further polarize public opinion and prejudice the jury. The very act of prosecuting a future president – someone positioned at the apex of political power – carries with it a level of societal weight that potentially impacts the proceedings far beyond the realm of purely legal considerations. This, inevitably, would add another layer to the analysis, influencing the strategy and approach of both sides involved.

The potential for appeals also demanded meticulous attention to every aspect of the legal proceedings. A conviction or acquittal, far from being a final resolution, could be challenged in higher courts, prompting renewed scrutiny of the evidence and procedures. Each decision of the judge, each ruling on admissibility, each piece of admitted evidence, would become a potential point of contention in future appeals. The meticulous documentation of every procedural step, the careful recording of every legal argument, and the complete preservation of all evidence were therefore not simply best practices but crucial aspects of the case's long-term legal viability. Both the prosecution and the defense would be working not only for the current trial, but also anticipating the potential for future legal battles and appeals. The stakes were not just about the current charges, but about the legacy and future reputation of all those involved. The legal battles were thus more than a simple contest; they were a complex interplay of legal strategy, political maneuvering, and the relentless pursuit of truth, or at least, the pursuit of what both sides considered to be the truth.

Investigation Phases and Key Decisions

Chapter Three

The investigation into the allegations against the president unfolded in distinct phases, each marked by crucial decisions that shaped the trajectory of the legal proceedings. Understanding these phases and the reasoning behind the key choices made is vital to comprehending the overall fairness and efficacy of the process. The initial phase, characterized by preliminary inquiries and fact-gathering, involved a complex interplay of investigative bodies, including law enforcement agencies and special prosecutors. This stage was critical in determining whether sufficient evidence existed to warrant a full-scale investigation and potential prosecution. The decision to initiate a formal investigation was not taken lightly, requiring a thorough evaluation of the credibility of the allegations and the availability of potential evidence. This often involved reviewing complaints, conducting initial interviews, and securing preliminary documentation. The weight of evidence at this stage, coupled with the potential political ramifications, heavily influenced the decision-making process. The absence of a clear and convincing threshold of evidence could have resulted in the case being dismissed prematurely, while an abundance of credible evidence might have warranted immediate and intensive investigative efforts.

The second phase focused on a more intensive examination of potential criminal activity. This typically involved the deployment of investigative resources, including forensic accountants, cybersecurity experts, and specialized law enforcement units. During this phase, investigators meticulously collected and analyzed evidence, often dealing with complex financial transactions, digital communications, and witness testimony. Key decisions made during this phase often revolved around resource allocation, investigative priorities, and the selection of appropriate investigative techniques. The strategic choices here could drastically impact the completeness and reliability of the overall investigation. For example, the decision to prioritize certain investigative leads over others, based on perceived strength of evidence or the availability of resources, could have long-lasting consequences for the case's outcome. Furthermore, the decision to utilize specific investigative techniques, such as wiretaps, undercover operations, or grand jury subpoenas, required careful legal and ethical consideration. Overly aggressive investigative tactics could risk violating the subject's due process rights and compromise the integrity of the investigation, whereas an insufficiently thorough approach could miss crucial evidence.

A third, crucial phase involved the decision to present the evidence to a grand jury. The grand jury, a body of citizens convened to determine whether sufficient evidence exists to indict an individual on criminal charges, played a pivotal role in evaluating the strength of the case against the president. The decision of what evidence to present to the grand jury, and the manner in which it was presented, represented a crucial juncture. The prosecution team had to carefully balance the need to present a compelling case while adhering to legal standards of evidence and avoiding the introduction of potentially prejudicial information. The grand jury's decision—to indict or not indict—had significant implications for the future course of the proceedings. An indictment would signify that the grand jury believed there was probable cause to believe the president had committed a crime, thereby triggering a criminal trial.

Conversely, a failure to indict could potentially bring the legal proceedings to an end, leaving unresolved questions about the president's conduct and raising concerns about the effectiveness of the justice system. This stage highlights the interplay between the legal process and public perception, with the grand jury's decision being subject to intense scrutiny and interpretation from the media and the public alike.

The subsequent trial phase, if the grand jury indicted, brought the case into the public arena. This phase involved the meticulous presentation of evidence in a court of law, including witness testimonies, physical evidence, and expert analysis. Key decisions during the trial centered on strategic legal arguments, the selection of witnesses, and the overall approach to presenting the evidence. The prosecution's task involved proving beyond a reasonable doubt that the president committed the alleged crimes, while the defense sought to discredit the prosecution's evidence and raise doubts about the guilt of the accused. The judge's rulings on evidentiary matters, the admissibility of evidence, and the management of the trial process played a vital role in shaping the proceedings. Each decision made by the judge could significantly affect the course of the trial and potentially influence the jury's verdict. This underscores the importance of judicial impartiality and the application of established legal procedures.

The trial's outcome, either a conviction or acquittal, would be followed by the potential for appeals. If the president was convicted, the defense team might appeal the verdict, raising various legal grounds for challenging the outcome. This could include claims of procedural errors, inadmissibility of evidence, or jury bias. The appeals process often involved a prolonged review of the trial record, with the appellate court determining whether any legal errors occurred that could have affected the fairness of the trial. The appellate court's decision could lead to a retrial, modification of the sentence, or affirmation of the original verdict. The entire appeals process, while potentially lengthy and complex, served as a critical safeguard against miscarriage of justice, ensuring that the legal process was fair and impartial, even when involving high-profile individuals. This post-trial phase further underscores the complexity of the legal system and the importance of adhering to established due process guarantees.

Throughout the investigation and legal proceedings, the decisions made at each stage were not only guided by legal principles but also impacted by the prevailing political climate. Public opinion, media coverage, and partisan divides could influence the decisions made by investigators, prosecutors, judges, and even jurors. This illustrates the inherent challenges of navigating the intersection of law, politics, and public perception, particularly in high-profile cases involving a sitting or former president. The analysis of these factors provides a deeper understanding of how the pursuit of justice operates within a complex political context. The political ramifications, both for the individuals involved and the broader political landscape, significantly influenced the dynamics of the entire process.

Finally, the investigation phases and key decisions highlighted the complexities of applying the legal process in such a sensitive context. The interplay between investigative techniques, evidentiary standards, legal arguments, and the political realities provided numerous challenges that demanded both meticulous legal expertise and careful consideration of ethical and public perception aspects. This intricate dance between legal rigor and political pressure is a hallmark of high-stakes cases, particularly those involving powerful figures. The entire process exemplifies the vital importance of upholding due process and ensuring a fair and equitable application of the law, even under immense public scrutiny and political pressure. The meticulous examination of each phase and every decision is crucial for a thorough understanding of the justice system's effectiveness and the extent to which it met the demands of fairness in a highly charged political environment. The ultimate goal of the investigation was not simply to determine guilt or innocence but also to uphold the principles of due process and ensure accountability within the constraints of the legal system.

Grand Jury Proceedings and Indictments

The transition from the preliminary investigation to the grand jury phase marked a significant escalation in the legal proceedings against the future president. This stage, shrouded in secrecy, plays a crucial role in determining whether sufficient evidence exists to proceed with a formal criminal trial. The grand jury, a body of citizens convened by the court, operates under a different set of rules and procedures compared to a public trial. Its primary function is not to determine guilt or innocence, but rather to assess whether there is probable cause to believe a crime has been committed and whether the accused should be formally charged.

Unlike a trial, grand jury proceedings are conducted in secret. The accused typically does not have the right to be present, nor does he have the right to confront witnesses or present evidence. The prosecutor presents evidence to the grand jury, which may include witness testimony, documents, and physical evidence. The defense is excluded from this process, creating an inherent imbalance of power that has been a source of ongoing debate amongst legal scholars. The secrecy surrounding these proceedings is intended to protect the rights of both the accused and potential witnesses. It prevents premature public disclosure of potentially damaging information that might compromise the fairness of a subsequent trial or harm the reputations of individuals who have not been formally charged with a crime. However, this secrecy also raises concerns about transparency and potential for abuse.

The evidence presented to the grand jury in this case was undoubtedly extensive and complex. It likely encompassed a wide array of materials gathered during the preceding investigative phases, including financial records, emails, testimony from individuals with firsthand knowledge of the alleged activities, and expert analysis to interpret complex financial transactions. The prosecutor's task was to present this evidence in a way that convinced the grand jury that there was probable cause to believe that crimes had been committed. This requires meticulous organization and a persuasive narrative that highlights the incriminating aspects of the evidence while mitigating any potential counter-arguments.

The role of the prosecutor in grand jury proceedings is crucial. They act as the sole legal advisor to the grand jury, guiding the jurors through the complexities of the legal process and the evidence presented. They have considerable discretion in determining what evidence to present and how to present it, influencing the grand jury's decision significantly. Critics argue that this imbalance of power allows prosecutors to essentially "shop" for indictments, selectively choosing evidence that supports their case while ignoring or downplaying evidence that might exculpate the accused. While the prosecutor's role is essential for the efficient function of the grand jury, the inherent potential for bias and manipulation necessitates ongoing vigilance to ensure the integrity of the process.

The grand jury's deliberations, though conducted in secrecy, follow a specific procedure. They typically hear evidence and testimony over several sessions, allowing them to thoroughly assess the merits of the case. Jurors have the opportunity to ask questions of witnesses and request additional information. Once the presentation of evidence is complete, the grand jury deliberates in private to reach a decision. This decision, whether to issue an indictment or not, is typically reached by a majority vote. A failure to reach a consensus, commonly known as a "no bill", would signify a lack of sufficient evidence to justify proceeding with an indictment.

The decision of the grand jury carries significant weight. An indictment, a formal accusation of a crime, signifies that the grand jury has found probable cause to believe that a crime has been committed and that the accused should stand trial. It represents a crucial threshold in the criminal justice system. The indictment itself does not establish guilt; it merely initiates the formal criminal proceedings. The actual determination of guilt or innocence rests with a trial jury, subject to the rigorous standards of proof required in a court of law.

However, an indictment carries considerable political and reputational consequences, particularly for a high-profile figure like the future president. Even if ultimately acquitted at trial, the accusation itself can significantly damage a person's public image and reputation. It also impacts their ability to conduct their business, both personal and professional, and can expose them to extensive legal costs and the emotional toll of enduring a long and often adversarial legal battle. This aspect underlines the importance of the grand jury's decision-making process and the imperative for it to be as fair and impartial as possible.

The potential for bias in grand jury proceedings, while acknowledged, remains a subject of ongoing legal and political debate. Some argue that the inherent imbalance of power, with the prosecution controlling the presentation of evidence and the defense excluded entirely, inherently favors the prosecution. Others point to the potential for prosecutorial overreach, where a prosecutor might pursue an indictment even if the evidence is weak or inconclusive, driven by political motivations or ambitions. These concerns underscore the need for rigorous oversight and transparent procedures to maintain the integrity of the grand jury system.

Furthermore, the composition of the grand jury itself can influence its decisions. A lack of diversity in the grand jury pool could lead to biases that impact the outcome of the deliberations. Concerns have been raised over the possibility that a grand jury might be more or less inclined to issue an indictment depending on the political affiliations or social backgrounds of its members. Ensuring a truly representative grand jury is crucial to fostering public trust in the impartiality of the legal system. The selection process and the overall composition of the grand jury deserve continuous scrutiny to guarantee equitable application of the law.

The eventual outcome of the grand jury proceedings in this case—whether indictments were issued and the specific charges levied—would significantly shape the subsequent trajectory of the legal and political landscape. The consequences of an indictment would extend far beyond the immediate legal ramifications, impacting public perception, political alliances, and the overall trajectory of the future president's career. The meticulous documentation and subsequent analysis of this phase are critical for understanding the intricacies of the process and its potential impacts on both the individual and the larger political sphere. The historical record demands a complete account of these events, including the evidence presented, the arguments made, and the ultimate conclusions reached by the grand jury. This narrative element not only enhances the factual accuracy of the account but also provides readers with the critical context necessary for a thorough understanding of the ensuing legal battles and their wider political reverberations. The thorough investigation into this phase, therefore, is essential for constructing a balanced and informed narrative, enabling readers to form their own informed conclusions about the events and their significance.

The handling of evidence before the grand jury, including its admissibility and the weight assigned to it, was another pivotal aspect of this phase. The rules of evidence are more relaxed in grand jury proceedings compared to a public trial; however, this doesn't eliminate the significance of the evidentiary standards. The prosecution had a responsibility to present credible and legally sound evidence. Examining the specific pieces of evidence presented, their origins, and the manner in which they were presented to the grand jury is crucial for a comprehensive analysis of this stage. The detailed scrutiny of this evidence, coupled with an understanding of the prosecutorial strategies employed, will illuminate the legal and strategic considerations that shaped the grand jury's eventual decision.

This detailed examination of the grand jury proceedings highlights the complexities of the legal system's handling of high-profile cases, particularly those with significant political implications. The interplay of legal process, political maneuvering, and public opinion underscores the importance of transparency, accountability, and a commitment to due process in all aspects of the legal system, especially when powerful figures are involved. The intricacies of this stage, from the selection of the grand jury itself to the handling of evidence and the decision-making process, demonstrate the need for a thorough, unbiased review of every step. This investigation aims to provide that in-depth analysis, offering the reader a clear understanding of this crucial phase in the unfolding narrative and its profound impact on the subsequent course of events. The thoroughness of this analysis serves not just as a historical record but as a crucial contribution to the understanding of the intersection between law, politics, and the public image of powerful individuals.

Trial Procedures and Legal Strategies

The grand jury's indictment marked the beginning of a protracted and highly publicized legal battle. The trial itself, anticipated with breathless anticipation by the media and the public alike, unfolded under the intense scrutiny of a nation. The prosecution, armed with a mountain of evidence painstakingly gathered during the preceding investigations, presented their case methodically, aiming to prove beyond a reasonable doubt the future president's guilt on all counts. Their legal strategy was multifaceted, combining direct evidence—such as financial records, witness testimonies, and physical artifacts—with circumstantial evidence that aimed to paint a comprehensive picture of a criminal conspiracy. The prosecution team, composed of seasoned federal prosecutors known for their rigorous approach to high-profile cases, adopted a strategy of building a narrative that meticulously connected the accused to each alleged crime. They carefully sequenced the presentation of evidence, starting with the foundational elements of each alleged offense, gradually building towards a compelling narrative of criminal intent and action.

Their opening statements set the tone, clearly outlining the charges and promising to present irrefutable proof of guilt. The meticulous organization of their case and their clear presentation of complex financial transactions and legal concepts were highly effective in keeping the jury engaged and focused. They employed expert witnesses, including forensic accountants, financial analysts, and law enforcement professionals, to explain the intricacies of the alleged schemes and provide credible interpretations of the evidence. These experts helped break down complex financial maneuvers, translating them into plain language understandable to the jury. Their testimony was vital in establishing the credibility of the prosecution's case, reinforcing their claim that the alleged crimes were not merely misunderstandings or unintentional errors but rather deliberate acts of criminal behavior. The cross-examination of the prosecution's witnesses by the defense was often aggressive, challenging the credibility of testimony and attempting to expose potential biases or inconsistencies.

The defense, facing a formidable opponent, employed a counter-strategy aimed at discrediting the prosecution's case and casting doubt on the evidence presented. Their central argument revolved around the lack of direct evidence linking the future president to the alleged criminal acts. They argued that the prosecution's case relied heavily on circumstantial evidence and the testimony of potentially biased witnesses. The defense team, comprised of renowned legal eagles known for their aggressive defense tactics and strategic maneuvering, meticulously dissected every piece of evidence presented by the prosecution. They challenged the chain of custody of certain exhibits, questioned the methodologies used by forensic accountants, and pointed to gaps in the prosecution's narrative. They employed a multi-pronged approach, including arguments focusing on the insufficiency of evidence, the potential for prosecutorial misconduct, and the credibility of witnesses.

They highlighted inconsistencies in witness testimony, challenged the accuracy of forensic analyses, and introduced alternative explanations for the financial transactions at the heart of the case. Their cross-examination aimed to expose vulnerabilities in the prosecution's evidence and sow seeds of doubt in the minds of the jury. The defense also employed expert witnesses of their own, offering alternative interpretations of the financial data and challenging the conclusions reached by the prosecution's experts. These expert witnesses provided counter-analysis of the financial documents, presenting alternative perspectives on the

meaning of the transactions and suggesting other plausible explanations for the accused's actions. The defense's strategy relied heavily on undermining the credibility of the prosecution's witnesses, pointing out potential biases, inconsistencies in their testimonies, and suggesting motives for them to provide false or misleading information.

A key aspect of the legal proceedings was the battle over the admissibility of evidence. Both sides engaged in lengthy pre-trial motions, arguing over the relevance, authenticity, and probative value of specific pieces of evidence. The judge, faced with complex legal arguments and a mountain of evidentiary materials, carefully considered each motion, ruling on the admissibility of various pieces of evidence. His rulings shaped the flow of the trial, dictating which evidence the jury was allowed to consider in their deliberations. These rulings often became focal points of debate, highlighting the intricate dance between the law and legal strategy. The prosecution's challenge lay in presenting a clear, compelling narrative supported by legally admissible evidence. The defense, conversely, had to overcome a large amount of evidence already deemed admissible, requiring a careful strategy of chipping away at its credibility, focusing on inconsistencies, raising doubts, and presenting alternative narratives.

The trial itself lasted for several months, featuring numerous witnesses, hours of testimony, and a massive amount of documentary evidence. The courtroom became a battleground of legal maneuvering, with both sides employing sophisticated techniques to sway the jury. The media coverage was intense, with daily updates and analyses dominating news cycles. The political implications were ever-present, influencing public opinion and shaping the narrative surrounding the trial. The arguments presented by both sides were intricate and complex, touching upon constitutional law, financial regulations, and criminal procedure. The use of legal precedent, the interpretation of statutes, and the application of case law constituted significant aspects of the legal arguments, often showcasing the nuances of the American legal system. The defense's strategy included employing tactics aimed at delaying the proceedings, introducing irrelevant information to confuse the jury, and questioning the credibility of the prosecution's key witnesses. They leveraged every available procedural tool to challenge the prosecution's case and to maximize their chances of achieving a favorable outcome.

The closing arguments provided both sides a final opportunity to summarize their case and address the jury directly. The prosecution reiterated the strength of their evidence, emphasizing the interconnectedness of the alleged crimes and the accused's clear culpability. They focused on the weight of the evidence, the consistency of the witnesses' accounts, and the clear pattern of criminal behavior revealed by their investigation. The defense, in their closing statements, revisited their central argument, again casting doubt on the credibility of the prosecution's case and highlighting the absence of direct evidence linking the future president to the alleged offenses. They appealed to the jury's sense of fairness and due process, emphasizing the importance of not convicting someone based on conjecture or circumstantial evidence. The defense's strategy was to leave the jury with reasonable doubt, urging them not to rush to judgment and to consider the potential for error or bias in the prosecution's case.

After weeks of deliberation, the jury delivered its verdict. The outcome, irrespective of its nature, had far-reaching implications, not only for the future president's career but also for the broader understanding of accountability and the rule of law within the American political system. The trial's impact transcended the immediate legal consequences, shaping public discourse and influencing future legal proceedings involving high-profile figures. The meticulous examination of the evidence, the legal maneuvering, and the intensity of the media scrutiny collectively served as a microcosm of the American justice system's strengths and challenges, highlighting the importance of due process, the complexities of high-stakes litigation, and the critical role of the jury in safeguarding fundamental rights. The detailed analysis of the legal arguments and strategies deployed in this trial offers a valuable insight into the workings of the American justice system, its capacity to handle cases of great political significance, and the enduring tension between legal principles and political realities. Regardless of the verdict, the trial left an indelible mark on the public consciousness, underscoring the importance of transparency, accountability, and an unwavering commitment to upholding the rule of law. The lessons learned from this intricate and high-stakes legal battle serve as a testament to the strength and resilience of the American legal system, even in the face of significant political pressure and public scrutiny. The case itself, therefore, continues to be a subject of intense discussion and analysis, shaping the ongoing debate about the intersection of law, politics, and public accountability.

Judicial Decisions and Rulings

The jury's verdict, whatever it may have been, served as the first domino in a cascade of legal challenges and appeals. The defense team, far from conceding defeat, immediately initiated post-trial motions, arguing for a mistrial based on alleged prosecutorial misconduct, juror bias, and the inadmissibility of certain pieces of evidence. These motions, meticulously documented and supported by extensive legal precedent, were carefully crafted to exploit any perceived weaknesses in the prosecution's case or procedural irregularities during the trial. The judge, presiding over the case with remarkable patience and impartiality, carefully considered each motion, meticulously reviewing the transcripts, evidence, and legal arguments presented by both sides. The scrutiny applied to these post-trial motions underscored the fundamental importance of due process and the rigorous standards required to ensure fairness and impartiality within the judicial system. The judge's rulings, delivered with clear and concise reasoning, became a crucial component in shaping the subsequent trajectory of the legal proceedings.

The initial rulings on the post-trial motions set the stage for further legal maneuvering. The defense's appeal to a higher court focused on the interpretation of key pieces of evidence, arguing that the jury's interpretation was flawed and that the prosecution had failed to prove guilt beyond a reasonable doubt. The appeals process, a hallmark of the American justice system, provided an opportunity for a more thorough review of the case, with a panel of judges examining the lower court's rulings and the entire body of evidence presented at trial. This process, often lengthy and complex, involved a meticulous examination of legal arguments, judicial precedent, and the nuances of legal interpretation. The appellate court's decision, meticulously reasoned and supported by a detailed analysis of the case, became a significant legal precedent, clarifying the application of specific laws and setting a standard for future cases with similar circumstances.

The appellate court's decision, while significant, did not necessarily mark the end of the legal journey. Further appeals could be lodged, potentially escalating the case to the highest court in the land – the Supreme Court. The Supreme Court's intervention, however, was contingent on whether the case presented a question of significant constitutional importance or a conflict in legal interpretation between different circuit courts. The possibility of a Supreme Court review added another layer of complexity to the case, underscoring the multi-layered nature of the American judicial system and the rigorous process involved in resolving high-stakes legal disputes. The prospect of Supreme Court involvement inherently raises questions about the intersection of law and politics, as such decisions can have far-reaching implications on legal interpretation and the very fabric of American jurisprudence. The sheer possibility of such a review added weight to the case, emphasizing the importance of legal precision and the thoroughness required at each stage of the judicial process.

The judicial decisions and rulings in this case weren't confined to the courtroom; they reverberated throughout the legal and political spheres, influencing future legal interpretations and shaping public discourse on issues of accountability, due process, and the intersection between law and politics. Legal scholars meticulously analyzed the rulings, dissecting the legal reasoning, identifying potential implications for future cases, and debating the broader societal impact of the decisions. Their analyses, published in scholarly journals and legal commentaries, contributed to a deeper understanding of the case and its potential ramifications on future legal precedents. The scholarly discourse surrounding these rulings transcended mere legal analysis; it provided crucial context and insight into the social, political, and cultural implications of the decisions, enriching the public's understanding of the legal process and the complexities of American justice.

The media played a significant role in disseminating information about the judicial decisions and shaping public opinion. News reports, opinion pieces, and televised analyses dissected the rulings, providing various perspectives and interpretations. The media's role, however, was not without its complexities. While it served as a vital conduit of information, its potential to influence public perception and to oversimplify complex legal issues could not be overlooked. The need for balanced reporting and careful analysis of judicial rulings was paramount, given the potential for the media to amplify biases or distort the nuanced understanding of legal proceedings.

The impact of these judicial decisions extended beyond legal circles and the media; they also influenced subsequent political debates and actions. The rulings served as a backdrop for political discourse, shaping discussions on campaign finance reform, ethics in government, and the very definition of political accountability. The decisions themselves became a catalyst for further legislative action and policy changes aimed at strengthening regulations, improving transparency, and enhancing ethical standards within the political system. This interaction between judicial rulings, political discourse, and legislative action underscored the interconnected nature of law, politics, and governance in a democratic society.

In examining the totality of the judicial decisions and rulings in this high-stakes case, a pattern emerges. The rulings highlighted the importance of due process in safeguarding individual rights, even when facing high-profile accusations. Each decision, from the

initial post-trial motions to any potential Supreme
Court review, provided further insight into the legal
complexities involved. These rulings, though
rendered within a specific legal context, contributed
to a broader, evolving understanding of the American
justice system, its strengths, its limitations, and its
ongoing adaptation to a constantly changing social
and political landscape. The rigorous application of
legal principles, the meticulous examination of
evidence, and the careful consideration of legal
arguments demonstrated the strength of the system,
while the potential for appeals and higher court
reviews highlighted the importance of checks and
balances within the judicial process. The transparency
of the process, subject to public scrutiny and media
attention, served as a testament to the underlying
principles of accountability and the rule of law that
underpin American democracy.

Furthermore, the case, and its resulting judicial
decisions, fueled an important discussion on the role
of the media in legal proceedings. The intense media
coverage, both during the trial and in the aftermath of
the rulings, brought the issues to the forefront of
national debate. The balance between the public's
right to know and the need to maintain the integrity of
the judicial process became a pivotal point of
contention. The case became a case study in the
delicate dance between transparency and the
preservation of a fair trial, raising questions about

media responsibility, the potential for biased reporting, and the effects of pervasive media coverage on public perception and jury selection in future high-profile trials. The discussion spurred further analysis of media ethics and the role of journalism in a democratic society grappling with the complexities of balancing public interest and the fairness of legal proceedings.

In conclusion, the judicial decisions and rulings in this case represent far more than a mere legal resolution to a high-profile legal battle; they serve as a complex tapestry woven from threads of legal interpretation, political maneuvering, and media scrutiny. The decisions themselves became pivotal points in the ongoing conversation about accountability, due process, and the delicate balance between law and politics. The meticulous review of the evidence, the intense legal battles, and the subsequent appeals represent the intricate workings of the American justice system at its highest levels. The analysis of these decisions offers a valuable insight not only into the specifics of the case but also into the broader themes of justice, fairness, and the enduring power of the rule of law in a society grappling with complex legal and political realities. The legacy of these rulings will undoubtedly continue to shape future legal discourse, ensuring that the case remains a significant touchstone in the ongoing evolution of American jurisprudence.

Appeals and Post Trial Developments

The judge's rulings on the post-trial motions, while meticulously reasoned, were far from the final word. The defense team, anticipating this, had already begun preparing for the next stage: the appeals process. The grounds for appeal were numerous and multifaceted, mirroring the complexity of the case itself. They argued that the judge had erred in admitting certain pieces of evidence, claiming they were prejudicial and irrelevant to the charges. The defense also challenged the jury selection process, alleging that the prosecution had systematically excluded potential jurors who might be sympathetic to the defendant, thereby creating an unfairly biased jury pool. This argument rested on statistical analysis of the jury selection process, comparing the demographics of the selected jury to the demographics of the wider community. The defense's experts presented compelling evidence of systematic exclusion, highlighting a disparity that suggested intentional bias on the part of the prosecution.

Furthermore, the appeal focused on the prosecution's summation, alleging that it contained inflammatory rhetoric designed to prejudice the jury against the defendant. Specific instances were highlighted, where the prosecution's language was deemed to have strayed beyond permissible advocacy and into the realm of personal attacks, attempting to sway the jury through emotional appeals rather than reasoned argument. The defense argued that this misconduct influenced the jury's deliberations, undermining the fairness of the trial. This section of the appeal heavily relied on transcripts of the trial, meticulously analyzing each phrase, tone, and inflection to demonstrate the inflammatory nature of the prosecution's closing arguments. Legal precedent regarding the acceptable bounds of prosecutorial rhetoric in closing statements was extensively cited, demonstrating clear violations that warranted a new trial.

The appeal also addressed procedural irregularities, particularly concerning the handling of witness testimony and the admissibility of expert opinions. The defense argued that certain witnesses were improperly questioned and coerced, leading to testimony that was unreliable and potentially false. The appeal did not suggest that these witnesses knowingly lied but that the methods used by the prosecution to extract information were potentially unethical and could have coerced the witnesses into providing misleading statements. This required an intricate legal analysis of the questioning techniques, comparing them to established standards of prosecutorial conduct and demonstrating instances where the prosecution's methods strayed from acceptable procedures. This section drew heavily upon legal scholarship and case law focusing on witness coercion and the integrity of testimony.

Similarly, the admissibility of expert testimony was challenged. The defense argued that the prosecution's experts lacked the necessary credentials to render opinions on certain crucial aspects of the case, their testimonies being based on speculative hypotheses rather than solid scientific or factual foundations. The appeal meticulously scrutinized the qualifications of the experts and the methodology behind their opinions, comparing them against prevailing legal standards for the admissibility of expert testimony in criminal cases.

The appellate court, a panel of experienced judges, carefully considered the arguments presented by both sides. The process was not a mere re-hearing of the trial; rather, it involved an in-depth analysis of the legal proceedings, focusing on procedural issues and errors of law. The appellate judges reviewed transcripts, legal briefs, and other materials, weighing the arguments of the defense against the response from the prosecution. The appellate judges were particularly interested in evidence of prosecutorial misconduct. They scrutinized the prosecution's methods to ensure that the defendant's rights to a fair trial were upheld. The appellate process is an integral part of the American judicial system, designed to ensure that justice is not only done but is seen to be done. This process involves a thorough review of the lower court's procedures, with specific focus on identifying any errors that may have materially affected the outcome of the trial.

The appellate court's decision, issued after months of deliberation, was a complex document that addressed each of the defense's arguments in detail. The court upheld the lower court's verdict on some points, finding the defense's arguments to be without merit. For instance, certain objections about the evidence presented were deemed to be tactical arguments made by the defense, rather than genuine breaches of procedural rules. However, the court did find merit in some of the defense's claims concerning the prosecution's summation and the handling of specific witness testimonies. The court determined that certain statements made during the prosecution's closing argument had indeed crossed the line into inflammatory rhetoric and constituted prosecutorial misconduct. They also found that the methods used to obtain testimony from certain witnesses were questionable and potentially coercive.

This led to the crucial decision: the appellate court ordered a retrial. This was a significant setback for the prosecution, highlighting the importance of adhering to strict legal procedures. The decision underscored the principle that a fair trial is paramount, regardless of the perceived guilt or innocence of the defendant. The retrial itself offered a new phase in the legal saga, requiring a re-examination of all aspects of the case, from witness testimony to evidence admissibility. The retrial highlighted the ongoing challenges in balancing the pursuit of justice with the unwavering need to uphold procedural fairness. The impact of the appellate court's decision extended beyond the immediate legal consequences. It set a legal precedent that had implications for future cases and underscored the importance of adherence to legal standards in all stages of the judicial process.

The political ramifications were equally significant. The decision to order a retrial created considerable uncertainty, influencing public opinion and raising questions about the integrity of the legal process. The media extensively covered the appeal and the retrial, shaping public perception and contributing to the ongoing political discourse surrounding the defendant. The case became a focal point for debates about the role of the justice system in a democratic society and the importance of ensuring fair and impartial trials, even for high-profile individuals.

The retrial itself, however, played out differently. Perhaps learning from the errors of the first trial, the prosecution adopted a more measured approach, avoiding inflammatory rhetoric and demonstrating greater attention to procedural correctness. The defense, in turn, sharpened its strategic focus, highlighting inconsistencies in the prosecution's case and carefully crafting its arguments to avoid the pitfalls that had characterized the first trial. The outcome of the retrial will depend on the presentation of evidence and the interpretation of the judge and the jury. The entire process, from the initial trial through the appeals process and the retrial, is a long and complex journey in the pursuit of justice. Every step is scrutinized, debated, and analyzed by legal experts, political commentators, and the public. The eventual outcome is not only a legal resolution but also a statement about the effectiveness of the legal system and its capacity to deliver justice. Regardless of the final verdict, the case continues to serve as a significant case study in American jurisprudence, highlighting the intricacies of the legal system and the constant struggle to balance justice with due process. The sheer volume of legal filings, the extensive media coverage, and the continuing public debate underscore the monumental significance of this case and its lasting impact on the American legal and political landscape.

Political Climate and Polarization

Chapter Four

The allegations against the president didn't exist in a vacuum; they unfolded against a backdrop of intense political polarization and a deeply divided nation. The very fabric of American society seemed frayed, with partisan divides sharper than perhaps at any point since the Civil War. This climate significantly influenced public perception of the accusations, often coloring interpretations through pre-existing political allegiances. Understanding this context is crucial to grasping the complexities of the situation and avoiding simplistic narratives.

The nation was, and remains, sharply divided along ideological lines. The traditional liberal-conservative spectrum had become less of a continuum and more of a chasm, with little common ground remaining on many key issues. This polarization wasn't merely a matter of differing policy preferences; it had seeped into the very foundations of trust and civil discourse. News sources, once considered relatively neutral arbiters of information, were increasingly viewed through partisan lenses. Cable news networks, in particular, catered to specific audiences, often reinforcing existing biases rather than challenging them with balanced reporting. The rise of social media further exacerbated the problem, creating echo chambers where individuals were primarily exposed to information confirming their own beliefs, while dissenting viewpoints were often marginalized or dismissed outright.

This intense polarization directly impacted the reception of the allegations. Supporters of the president tended to view the accusations as politically motivated attacks, part of a broader effort to undermine his administration. They often questioned the credibility of the sources and expressed concerns about the fairness of the legal process. Conversely, opponents of the president readily accepted the accusations as evidence of wrongdoing, often interpreting any attempts to defend him as evidence of a cover-up. The initial media coverage reflected this division, with different outlets framing the allegations in starkly contrasting ways. Some presented the accusations as serious crimes demanding immediate investigation, while others portrayed them as politically motivated smears designed to damage the president's reputation.

The lack of trust in established institutions, including the media and the judiciary, further complicated the situation. Many Americans, regardless of their political affiliation, expressed cynicism towards the government and its institutions. This distrust manifested in various ways, from skepticism about the motives of investigators to questioning the impartiality of judges and juries. The erosion of public trust in these institutions made it harder to reach consensus on the facts of the case and its implications.

Public opinion polls and surveys conducted throughout the period of the allegations reflected this deep division. While some polls showed a significant percentage of the population believing the president had committed wrongdoing, others indicated substantial support for him, with many dismissing the accusations as politically driven. The results varied widely depending on the polling methodology, the sampling of respondents, and even the wording of the questions themselves. This inconsistency further highlighted the challenge of obtaining a clear and objective understanding of public opinion in such a polarized environment.

The impact on the president's approval ratings was significant, though not entirely consistent. While the allegations undoubtedly caused some erosion in his approval ratings, the extent of the decline varied depending on factors such as the intensity of media coverage, the release of new evidence, and the president's own public response. His most ardent supporters remained steadfast in their loyalty, while some who had previously supported him shifted their views in light of the accusations. This pattern highlighted the profound influence of pre-existing political attitudes on how the allegations were perceived and responded to.

The political fallout extended far beyond the president's immediate approval ratings. The allegations triggered heated debates within both political parties, revealing existing fractures and exacerbating tensions. The investigations, trials, and subsequent appeals became highly politicized events, further dividing the electorate. The very process of determining the truth became intertwined with political battles, with each side maneuvering for strategic advantage.

The allegations also had profound implications for the political landscape. They led to intensified partisan warfare, increased distrust in government, and a growing sense of national division. The consequences extended to other political contests, influencing elections at various levels and shaping debates on issues related to accountability, transparency, and the role of the media in a polarized society. The impact was far-reaching, highlighting how even isolated events could have cascading effects on the overall political climate.

Moreover, the case highlighted the vulnerability of democratic institutions to political manipulation and the dangers of unchecked polarization. The ease with which certain narratives could be amplified and disseminated through social media and partisan news outlets raised concerns about the integrity of the electoral process and the future of informed public discourse. The case served as a stark reminder of the importance of preserving faith in institutions and fostering a climate of trust and mutual respect.

The experience underscored the need for reforms to address the problem of political polarization and its impact on the fairness and integrity of political processes. The debate around these issues extends beyond this particular case, reflecting a wider concern about the ability of the nation to navigate the challenges posed by a deeply fractured society. These questions will continue to resonate for years to come, shaping the political discourse and influencing the direction of American politics. The very foundations of public trust in government and its institutions are at stake, requiring serious and sustained efforts to restore faith and ensure a healthy democratic process. The investigation, while centered on a single individual, ultimately exposed deep-seated vulnerabilities within the system itself. Only through a concerted effort towards dialogue, understanding, and meaningful institutional reform can the nation hope to bridge the widening divisions and safeguard its democratic ideals. The president's case, therefore, serves not only as a legal and political drama but as a cautionary tale about the perilous consequences of unchecked polarization.

Medias Role in Shaping Public Perception

The allegations against the president, however serious, did not exist in isolation. Their impact, their very meaning, was profoundly shaped by the way they were presented, interpreted, and disseminated through the media landscape. This wasn't a simple transmission of facts; it was a complex interplay of narrative construction, selective reporting, and the powerful influence of pre-existing biases within the media ecosystem. Understanding this media role is crucial to comprehending the public's response, the political ramifications, and ultimately, the enduring legacy of the entire affair.

The 24/7 news cycle, fueled by social media's instant dissemination, created a whirlwind of information and misinformation. The traditional news outlets, struggling to maintain relevance in a fragmented media environment, often found themselves competing with a deluge of unverified claims and emotionally charged opinions. This environment fostered a climate of "infotainment," where the pursuit of sensationalism sometimes overshadowed the pursuit of factual accuracy. The result was a public often overwhelmed and confused, struggling to distinguish between legitimate reporting and partisan spin.

One striking aspect of the media coverage was the clear partisan divide in its interpretation. Right-leaning outlets tended to downplay or outright dismiss the seriousness of the allegations, often focusing on what they framed as "political attacks" and "witch hunts." Conversely, left-leaning outlets emphasized the gravity of the accusations, sometimes presenting them in a way that amplified public outrage. This polarization within the media mirrored, and in turn exacerbated, the already deep partisan divisions within the country. It wasn't just a matter of differing interpretations; it was a battle for narrative control, each side seeking to frame the events to align with their pre-existing political agendas.

Independent journalism, though striving for objectivity, often found itself caught in the crossfire. Attempts at balanced reporting could be easily misinterpreted as tacit endorsement of one side or the other, leaving journalists vulnerable to accusations of bias regardless of their intent. The pressure to produce content quickly, to meet the demands of the relentless news cycle, sometimes compromised the depth and thoroughness of investigations. The resulting rush to judgment could lead to inaccurate reporting, further fueling public confusion and mistrust.

Furthermore, the rise of opinion-based programming and commentary blurred the lines between news and opinion. The constant stream of punditry and analysis, often lacking in nuance and balance, further contributed to the polarization of public opinion. Viewers and readers were bombarded with conflicting narratives, making it increasingly difficult to discern fact from opinion. This blurring of boundaries weakened the public's ability to critically assess information and form informed opinions. Instead of fostering an informed electorate, the media landscape often created an echo chamber, reinforcing pre-existing beliefs and deepening partisan divides.

The use of social media platforms added another layer of complexity. These platforms, while offering opportunities for direct engagement and citizen journalism, also became breeding grounds for misinformation and conspiracy theories. The rapid spread of false or misleading information, often amplified by algorithms designed to maximize engagement, contributed to the erosion of public trust in institutions, including the media itself. Fact-checking efforts

struggled to keep pace with the speed and scale of misinformation campaigns, further complicating the task of discerning truth from falsehood.

The use of inflammatory language and emotionally charged rhetoric by certain media outlets also played a significant role in shaping public perception. The use of terms like "scandal," "cover-up," and "betrayal" served to heighten the emotional response of the audience, often preempting rational deliberation and balanced analysis. This strategy aimed to mobilize support for a particular perspective by manipulating emotions rather than engaging in reasoned debate. The result was a public conversation dominated by feelings and accusations rather than facts and evidence.

The case study, therefore, transcends the specific allegations against the president; it represents a broader concern about the role of media in a polarized political climate. The media's ability to shape public opinion is undeniable. The question is whether this power is being wielded responsibly, whether the pursuit of truth and objectivity is prioritized above the pursuit of ratings and political advantage. The analysis compels a critical examination of media ethics and the need for greater media literacy among the public. Without a vigilant citizenry capable of discerning truth from falsehood, the potential for

manipulation and the erosion of democratic principles
is significant. The episode serves as a warning about
the fragility of truth in the age of instant information,
a reminder that informed citizenship demands critical
engagement with the media landscape and a
commitment to seeking verifiable facts from diverse
and reliable sources.

The long-term consequences of the media's role in
this case extend beyond the immediate political
fallout. The public's trust in institutions, particularly
those tasked with upholding the rule of law and
disseminating accurate information, suffered
significant damage. Restoring that trust requires a
multifaceted approach, including improved media
literacy programs, stricter accountability mechanisms
for misinformation, and a renewed commitment to
ethical journalism. It requires a conscious effort from
the media itself to prioritize accuracy, objectivity, and
responsible reporting over sensationalism and
partisan agendas.

The narrative presented by different media outlets
also impacted the legal processes. Public opinion,
fueled by media coverage, can influence jury
selection, witness testimony, and even judicial
decisions. The pressure of public perception,
especially in a highly polarized climate, can
undermine the integrity of the legal system itself. The
case highlighted the need for judicial independence
and the importance of safeguarding legal processes

from undue influence by the media or public opinion. The delicate balance between the public's right to know and the need to ensure a fair trial was severely tested.

The media's role in shaping public perception was not merely a passive reflection of existing political divisions; it actively shaped and amplified them. The media acted as a powerful force, reinforcing pre-existing biases, creating echo chambers, and contributing to the fragmentation of public discourse. The case stands as a crucial study in media's power to influence public opinion, highlighting both the opportunities and the dangers inherent in the media's role in a democratic society. It underscores the need for ongoing analysis, reform, and a renewed dedication to responsible information dissemination. The story's ultimate impact rests not just on the facts of the allegations themselves, but on the way those facts, or interpretations of them, were presented and consumed by a media-saturated public. The way forward requires a critical introspection by media organizations and a heightened awareness among the public to discern truth and resist manipulation. The fight for truth in a fragmented media landscape is a continuous one, requiring vigilance, critical thinking, and a commitment to informed citizenship.

Public Opinion Polls and Surveys

The media's portrayal of the allegations against the president, as we've seen, significantly influenced public perception. However, the media wasn't the sole determinant of public opinion. To gain a complete understanding, we must delve into the realm of public opinion polls and surveys conducted during and after the unfolding of the allegations. These surveys offer valuable insights into how the public perceived the accusations, their impact on the president's approval ratings, and the evolving dynamics of public trust and confidence. A thorough examination of these polls provides a critical counterpoint to the often-biased narratives presented by various media outlets, painting a more nuanced picture of the public's collective response.

Early polls, conducted in the immediate aftermath of the allegations surfacing, revealed a significant degree of uncertainty and division within the public. Many respondents expressed a lack of sufficient information to form a solid opinion, highlighting the impact of the initial media blitz, which often lacked context or presented conflicting narratives. This initial ambiguity underscores the crucial role of reliable information dissemination in shaping public perception. The polls revealed a clear correlation between media consumption patterns and initial opinions. Individuals who primarily consumed news from outlets known for their critical stance towards the president tended to express greater skepticism and condemnation, while those relying on more supportive media outlets often displayed more leniency or outright dismissal.

As more information emerged, both from official investigations and through investigative journalism, public opinion began to shift, albeit slowly and unevenly. The shifts weren't uniformly positive or negative, but rather reflected a complex interplay of factors. Some polls indicated an increase in negative sentiment towards the president, directly linked to the release of damning evidence or particularly damaging revelations. Conversely, other polls showed a hardening of partisan lines, with supporters of the president demonstrating unwavering faith despite the accusations, while opponents remained unconvinced, even in the face of ostensibly exonerating evidence. This polarization highlighted the deep-seated political divisions already present in society, divisions that the allegations served to amplify rather than resolve.

The methodologies employed by different polling organizations also played a significant role in shaping the interpretation of results. Variations in sampling techniques, question wording, and data analysis can lead to significantly different outcomes, emphasizing the importance of critically examining the methodology behind each survey. Polls conducted through telephone surveys, for instance, may exhibit biases due to limited reach, potentially excluding certain demographic segments. Online polls, while offering broader reach, can be vulnerable to manipulation and lack the rigorous sampling techniques of professionally conducted surveys. This highlights the crucial need for transparency and methodological rigor in conducting and interpreting public opinion polls, emphasizing the importance of using data from reputable and academically sound organizations.

Furthermore, the timing of the polls is critical. Polls conducted immediately after a significant development—such as a court hearing, the release of a report, or a major media exposé—may reflect immediate reactions that may not reflect long-term trends. For a complete understanding, it's vital to analyze the trend of opinion over time, tracking shifts and patterns across multiple surveys conducted at various intervals. By examining these longitudinal trends, researchers can better understand the duration and intensity of public opinion on specific issues, distinguishing between fleeting reactions and more sustained shifts in public sentiment. This longitudinal approach allows for a more informed interpretation of the data, reducing the risks associated with over-interpreting isolated snapshots in time.

Analyzing the demographic breakdowns within the polling data revealed further illuminating nuances. The president's approval ratings often varied significantly across different demographic groups, such as age, race, ethnicity, geographic location, and political affiliation. These differences underlined the complex and multifaceted nature of public opinion, highlighting how the impact of the allegations was not uniformly distributed across the population. Such disparities highlighted pre-existing societal divisions and emphasized how these were further amplified by the allegations, reinforcing existing political fault lines.

The influence of social media also deserves careful consideration. While traditional polls provided a snapshot of the broader public's sentiment, the rapidly evolving landscape of social media provided a real-time, albeit less rigorously controlled, window into public discourse. The volume and intensity of online discussions, particularly on platforms like Twitter and Facebook, offered valuable insights into the prevalent narratives, the key talking points, and the prevailing emotional tone surrounding the allegations. While anecdotal, the intensity and direction of online chatter often foreshadowed or mirrored trends observed in formal polling data, highlighting the symbiotic relationship between traditional media and social media in shaping public perception. The speed at which narratives could be constructed, amplified, and disseminated via social media also served to highlight the challenges faced in managing the flow of information and ensuring a fair and balanced representation of events.

Examining public opinion regarding the legal processes involved in the investigations revealed additional complexities. Public confidence in the integrity of the various institutions involved—ranging from law enforcement agencies to the judiciary—often fluctuated depending on developments in the case. Events such as the appointment of a special prosecutor, the release of investigative reports, and the unfolding of court proceedings directly affected public trust and perception of fairness. Polls tracking public confidence in these institutions provided critical insights into the impact of these events and the potential erosion or reinforcement of public faith in the rule of law. This impact was especially noteworthy considering the president's own role as the head of the executive branch, highlighting the potential for conflict of interest and the implications for democratic governance.

Finally, it's crucial to acknowledge the limitations of public opinion polls. They capture snapshots of sentiment at a specific point in time and are subject to methodological biases and sampling errors. While they provide valuable insights, they shouldn't be viewed as definitive measures of truth or justice. The human element—the complexities of individual beliefs, biases, and perspectives—cannot be fully captured by numerical data. Therefore, interpreting polling data requires careful consideration of context, methodology, and the inherent limitations of the polling process itself. It must be viewed as one piece of the puzzle, used in conjunction with other forms of evidence and analysis to construct a comprehensive understanding of the situation.

In conclusion, the public opinion polls and surveys conducted during this period offer a critical lens through which to examine the broader impact of the allegations against the president. They provide a multifaceted picture of public perception, revealing both the immediate and long-term consequences of the scandal. By considering the limitations of polling data alongside its strengths, and by analyzing the data in conjunction with other forms of evidence, a more complete and nuanced understanding of the interplay between law, politics, and public opinion emerges. This understanding is vital for assessing the lasting implications of the scandal on both the president's career and the American political landscape as a whole. The journey toward understanding the truth often requires navigating a complex maze of information and perspectives; public opinion polls, while not providing all the answers, offer a crucial piece of the map.

Impact on the Presidents Approval Ratings

The initial wave of allegations against the president sent shockwaves through the political landscape, immediately impacting his approval ratings. Pre-existing trends in public opinion, however, played a crucial role in shaping the severity of this impact. For instance, if his approval ratings were already low due to other policy decisions or controversies, the allegations might have caused a more dramatic decline. Conversely, if he enjoyed broad public support, the initial impact might have been less significant, potentially allowing for a recovery as the legal processes unfolded. Analyzing polling data from this period reveals a complex interplay of factors beyond the mere existence of the allegations themselves.

Numerous polling organizations, including Gallup, Pew Research Center, Quinnipiac University, and others, tracked the president's approval ratings closely. The immediate aftermath of the allegations saw a noticeable dip in his approval numbers across most polls. The magnitude of this dip varied based on the specific polling methodology, sample size, and the wording of the questions posed to respondents. This variability underscores a key challenge in interpreting polling data – the susceptibility to bias introduced through the survey design itself. Even seemingly minor variations in question phrasing can lead to substantial differences in the results, highlighting the need for a critical and nuanced approach to analyzing these figures.

Furthermore, demographic breakdowns within the polling data offer crucial insights. Changes in support among specific demographic groups – such as age, race, gender, or political affiliation – can provide a deeper understanding of the factors driving shifts in overall approval. For example, a significant drop in support among previously loyal demographic segments could indicate a deeper erosion of trust, suggesting a more profound and potentially long-lasting impact on the president's political standing. Conversely, if the decline in approval is concentrated among specific groups known for their opposition, it might suggest a hardening of partisan lines rather than a widespread loss of public confidence.

The evolution of public opinion after the initial shock is equally crucial. Did the president's approval ratings stabilize, decline further, or even show signs of recovery over time? Did the public's response correlate with specific events in the legal process, such as the filing of charges, the commencement of trials, or the release of new information? Tracking the trends over time, rather than focusing solely on immediate snapshots, offers a more holistic view of the long-term impact of the allegations. Analysis should incorporate not just the raw numbers but also the context surrounding those numbers – the political climate, the dominant media narratives, and any major policy decisions or events occurring concurrently.

It's important to acknowledge the limitations of polling data. Polling inherently reflects a snapshot in time and is susceptible to various biases, including sampling errors, question wording effects, and the respondent's own biases and motivations. The margin of error in polling data should always be considered, as it indicates the range within which the true population percentage likely falls. Over-reliance on a single poll or a small set of polls without considering their methodological differences can lead to inaccurate conclusions. Therefore, a robust analysis requires consulting data from multiple sources, cross-referencing findings, and recognizing the inherent limitations of each data set.

The impact on the president's approval ratings should be considered in conjunction with other indicators of his political standing. For example, changes in fundraising, campaign contributions, endorsements from key political figures, and the performance of his party in subsequent elections provide additional data points to assess the long-term consequences of the allegations. A decline in fundraising might signal a loss of investor confidence, impacting his ability to compete effectively in future elections. A shift in endorsements could indicate a weakening of his alliances within his own party or broader political network. Similarly, poor performance by his party in elections could serve as a barometer of the public's overall assessment of his leadership and his handling of the allegations.

Furthermore, the media's coverage of the polling data itself influences public opinion. The way in which the polls are reported, the emphasis on certain numbers versus others, and the accompanying narratives all shape how the public interprets the findings. Media bias, intentional or otherwise, can lead to a skewed presentation of the data, potentially impacting public sentiment beyond the objective figures themselves. Therefore, understanding the media landscape surrounding the polls is critical to evaluating the overall impact of the allegations and the public's evolving perception of the president.

Moreover, the context of the surrounding political climate deserves careful consideration. If the allegations emerged during a period of intense political polarization, the impact on the president's approval might be shaped by pre-existing partisan divides, with supporters largely unmoved and opponents even more firmly entrenched in their opposition. Similarly, the existence of other major political events, policy debates, or national crises could overshadow the impact of the allegations, potentially lessening their immediate impact on public opinion. In contrast, if the allegations surfaced during a period of relative political calm, they might have a more pronounced and immediate effect on public sentiment, lacking the mitigating influence of other significant issues.

The legal processes themselves – the timing, the evidence presented, the rulings of the courts, and the public's perception of the fairness and transparency of the legal proceedings – can significantly influence public opinion and the president's approval ratings. A protracted legal battle, with ongoing revelations and shifting narratives, can sustain public attention and continue to exert pressure on the president's standing. Public perceptions of fairness and impartiality in the legal process are also crucial; a sense that the process is unfair or biased can negatively affect public support, even if the legal outcome favors the president. Conversely, a speedy and transparent process that leads to a clear outcome can help to mitigate the long-term impact on his approval ratings.

Ultimately, understanding the impact of the allegations on the president's approval ratings requires a comprehensive analysis that combines polling data with an understanding of the political context, media coverage, legal proceedings, and the evolving dynamics of public opinion. This holistic approach allows for a more nuanced understanding of how these intertwined factors shaped public perception and the long-term consequences of the allegations on the president's career and the American political landscape. By moving beyond a simplistic correlation between allegations and approval ratings, and by examining the complex interplay of these factors, a more complete and accurate picture of the situation emerges. This, in turn, allows for a more informed discussion about the role of law, politics, and public opinion in shaping the leadership of a nation. The challenge, as always, lies in

separating the noise from the signal, navigating the biases inherent in both the data and the interpretations, and arriving at a grounded understanding based on evidence, analysis, and a healthy dose of skepticism.

Political Fallout and Consequences

The immediate shockwaves rippled outwards, far beyond the president's approval ratings. The allegations, regardless of their ultimate legal outcome, irrevocably altered the political landscape. The ongoing investigations, the constant media scrutiny, and the partisan battles that erupted in their wake created a climate of profound uncertainty. This uncertainty permeated every level of government, impacting policy-making, legislative processes, and international relations.

One of the most immediate consequences was the paralysis of legislative action. Crucial bills, essential for addressing pressing national issues, became entangled in the vortex of the scandal. Members of Congress, fearing political repercussions and torn along partisan lines, found it increasingly difficult to reach consensus on even the most non-controversial issues. The president's ability to negotiate and compromise, already weakened by the allegations, further deteriorated, leaving many important initiatives stalled. The resulting legislative gridlock frustrated both proponents and opponents of the president's policies, creating a sense of national malaise and undermining public trust in the government's ability to function effectively. This wasn't merely a matter of slowed progress; critical areas like infrastructure, healthcare reform, and economic stimulus packages all languished in this climate of political dysfunction. The sheer volume of energy devoted to the allegations and subsequent investigations diverted valuable time and resources from the substantive work of governance.

The impact extended beyond domestic policy. The allegations cast a long shadow over the nation's international standing. Foreign leaders, previously accustomed to dealing with a strong and decisive American president, now faced a figure shrouded in uncertainty and embroiled in scandal. The president's ability to project American power and influence on the global stage diminished significantly. Alliances were strained, negotiations became more difficult, and America's credibility in international forums suffered a measurable decline. The perception of instability at home translated directly into a weakened global leadership role for the United States, creating opportunities for rival nations to assert their influence and potentially undermining decades of carefully built international partnerships. Specific instances, such as stalled trade negotiations and hesitant responses to international crises, highlighted the real-world impact of the president's diminished political capital.

The political fallout also fueled a significant increase in political polarization. The allegations became yet another battleground in the ongoing culture war, further dividing the nation along already entrenched partisan lines. Supporters of the president rallied around him, fiercely defending his character and dismissing the allegations as politically motivated attacks. Opponents, on the other hand, saw the accusations as confirmation of their long-held suspicions about his character and fitness for office. The media played a crucial role in amplifying these divisions, with different outlets offering widely varying perspectives on the allegations and their significance. The result was an increasingly fragmented media landscape, where citizens often consumed information filtered through the lenses of their pre-existing beliefs and biases, making it difficult to establish common ground or a shared understanding of the facts. This entrenched polarization made constructive dialogue and compromise almost impossible, exacerbating the existing political gridlock and undermining the democratic

process itself. The president's own rhetoric, often inflammatory and divisive, contributed significantly to this environment of heightened polarization.

Beyond the immediate political turmoil, the long-term consequences of the allegations remained uncertain, casting a long shadow over the future of American politics. The erosion of public trust in government, already a significant concern before the scandal, deepened considerably. Citizens became more cynical about the political process, increasingly disillusioned with the ability of their elected officials to act in the public interest. Voter turnout potentially suffered as a result of this pervasive cynicism, further weakening the democratic system's legitimacy and efficacy. The scandal also raised profound questions about the nature of accountability for high-ranking officials, prompting debates about the effectiveness of existing mechanisms for investigating and prosecuting powerful individuals. Discussions regarding campaign finance reform, ethics in government, and the role of media in shaping public opinion intensified.

The allegations also had a significant impact on the funding of political campaigns and the influence of special interests. Donors, wary of associating themselves with a controversial figure, became more hesitant to provide financial support, potentially impacting the ability of both the president and his allies to fund future campaigns. Conversely, this financial uncertainty might have opened opportunities for rival candidates and political parties, altering the landscape of future elections. Furthermore, the scandal served as a potent reminder of the pervasive influence of money in politics, reigniting debates about campaign finance reform and the potential for corruption. This impact extends beyond financial contributions, encompassing the strategic alliances forged and broken in the wake of the allegations, demonstrating the complex interplay between political power and financial resources.

The impact on the judiciary was also profound. The allegations brought intense scrutiny to the legal processes themselves, raising questions about the fairness and impartiality of the legal system. The high-profile nature of the case and the involvement of powerful individuals attracted unprecedented levels of media attention and public debate, adding pressure on judges and legal professionals. Concerns about political bias within the justice system were amplified, leading to calls for increased transparency and accountability within the judiciary. The long-term effects of this increased scrutiny on public trust in the legal system remained to be seen, potentially affecting future cases and legal proceedings.

In conclusion, the political fallout from the allegations extended far beyond the immediate impact on the president's approval ratings. The scandal created a cascade of consequences that permeated the legislative, executive, and judicial branches of government, significantly impacting domestic and international policy, fueling political polarization, eroding public trust, and raising profound questions about the future of American democracy. The full extent of these long-term consequences remained to be seen, but it was clear that the allegations left an indelible mark on the nation's political landscape. The story of the allegations is not just about the president; it is about the fragility of democratic institutions, the complexities of public opinion, and the enduring power of political scandal to reshape the nation. The analysis of these events offers a valuable case study for future generations of political scientists, legal scholars, and journalists, highlighting the intricate interplay between law, politics, and public perception in the shaping of national destiny. The ongoing debate surrounding these events serves as a critical reminder of the constant vigilance required to protect and strengthen the foundations of a healthy democracy.

Similar Cases Involving High Profile Figures

Chapter Five

The case surrounding the President's alleged criminal activities, while unique in its specifics, resonates with a disturbingly familiar chord when viewed within the broader context of high-profile political scandals worldwide. The pattern of accusations—abuse of power, financial impropriety, conflicts of interest—is remarkably consistent across nations and political systems. A comparative analysis reveals unsettling parallels, highlighting the vulnerabilities inherent in systems of power and the persistent challenge of holding powerful individuals accountable.

One compelling parallel can be drawn to the numerous corruption cases that have plagued various European governments. The intricacies of campaign finance laws, often opaque and easily manipulated, have frequently been exploited by politicians to enrich themselves or gain an unfair advantage. Cases in Italy, involving complex webs of financial transactions and alleged collusion with organized crime, showcase the difficulty in untangling these schemes, particularly when powerful individuals are involved. The sheer complexity of these financial operations often requires extensive investigation and forensic accounting, precisely the challenges faced in the President's case. The use of shell companies and offshore accounts, a common tactic in these international cases, mirrors allegations leveled against the President, underscoring the transnational nature of such illicit activities. Similarly, investigations into alleged bribery and influence-peddling in several Eastern European countries offer a stark reminder of how political power can be leveraged for personal gain, often with devastating consequences for democratic institutions. The lack of transparency in these systems, mirroring concerns raised about the President's actions, often creates an environment where accountability is significantly diminished.

Across the Atlantic, several Latin American leaders have faced accusations of corruption, ranging from embezzlement of public funds to involvement in drug trafficking. These cases often expose the porousness of checks and balances within developing democracies, where institutions are weaker and the rule of law is more easily circumvented. The President's alleged abuse of power finds a disturbing echo in these instances, where the personal enrichment of leaders is often facilitated by a culture of impunity. The often-violent responses to investigations and attempts to obstruct justice in these countries parallel the allegations of resistance to inquiry in the President's case, highlighting a global trend of powerful individuals using their influence to evade accountability.

The comparison is not limited to developing nations. Even in established democracies, the line between legitimate political action and criminal behavior can be blurry, especially when it comes to campaign finance and lobbying. The United States itself has witnessed high-profile cases involving allegations of bribery, obstruction of justice, and abuse of power, demonstrating that this phenomenon is not unique to any particular political system. The Watergate scandal, for instance, remains a cautionary tale of the lengths to which political figures might go to protect their power and influence, a narrative that has unsettling similarities to the current situation. The subsequent investigations and legal battles exposed flaws in the system, particularly concerning oversight and accountability. Similarly, numerous cases involving campaign finance violations in the US underscore the vulnerability of the electoral process to manipulation and the need for stronger regulatory frameworks to maintain its integrity.

Further, the complexities involved in investigating and prosecuting high-profile figures are strikingly similar across various jurisdictions. The sheer resources required to mount a robust investigation, the political pressures that inevitably arise, and the challenges of obtaining unbiased witness testimony are all common themes. The difficulty in securing convictions, particularly when facing powerful individuals with access to high-priced legal counsel and influence within the judicial system, is a recurring challenge worldwide. This often leads to a sense of disillusionment among citizens who perceive that justice is not being served fairly, thereby undermining faith in institutions and exacerbating political polarization.

The international parallels also shed light on the importance of international cooperation in investigating and prosecuting transnational crimes. The President's case, if involving cross-border financial transactions or other elements of international reach, will highlight the need for improved mechanisms for information sharing and mutual legal assistance between nations. The existence of sophisticated international networks for money laundering and other financial crimes makes cross-border cooperation essential for effective enforcement. Examples from ongoing investigations into international tax evasion and organized crime demonstrate the significant challenges and successes in this area. The lessons learned from these global efforts can provide valuable insights into how best to proceed in the President's case, particularly regarding gathering evidence and securing international cooperation.

Furthermore, exploring international legal standards and practices surrounding similar accusations helps to establish a framework for evaluating the President's actions. Conventions against corruption, international human rights law, and the principles of due process provide a valuable benchmark for assessing the conduct of political figures and the adequacy of legal responses. Examining how other countries have addressed similar situations, including their legal frameworks and prosecutorial approaches, enables a more comprehensive understanding of the President's case and its implications for broader concepts of justice and accountability.

Moreover, a comparative analysis highlights the nuanced cross-cultural perspectives on leadership and accountability. What constitutes acceptable behavior in one political context might be viewed as egregious in another. Understanding these differing cultural norms is essential for a thorough assessment of the President's case and for avoiding ethnocentric biases in the analysis. Examining the varied cultural expectations regarding transparency, integrity, and the responsibilities of leaders can enrich the understanding of the accusations and their consequences. This necessitates considering the specific political and social contexts within which the President's actions occurred, rather than simply applying universal standards without understanding the underlying nuances of the cultural environment.

Ultimately, analyzing similar cases involving high-profile figures globally reveals that the challenges of accountability for those in power are not unique to the United States. The recurring patterns of abuse, obstruction, and evasion of justice underscore the urgent need for stronger institutional safeguards, enhanced transparency, and improved international cooperation to ensure that all individuals, regardless of their status or position, are held accountable under the law. The President's case serves as a potent case study within this larger global context, highlighting the enduring struggle for justice and accountability in the face of political power. The comparative analysis presented here aims not just to draw parallels but to illuminate the systemic issues that allow such scandals to occur repeatedly, prompting a critical reflection on how to prevent future occurrences and strengthen democratic institutions worldwide. The lessons learned from these international precedents provide a framework for understanding the complexities of the President's case and offer valuable guidance for ensuring greater accountability in the future.

International Legal Standards and Practices

The allegations against the President, however domestically focused, inevitably invite a comparative analysis within the broader framework of international legal standards and practices. While the specifics of US law and procedure differ from those of other nations, the underlying principles of accountability, due process, and the rule of law provide a crucial comparative lens. Examining how similar allegations have been handled in other jurisdictions, particularly those with robust legal systems and traditions of democratic governance, offers valuable insights into the strengths and weaknesses of the current processes.

One key area of comparison involves the concept of abuse of power. Many countries have specific legal provisions addressing this, ranging from general corruption statutes to more narrowly defined offenses related to bribery, embezzlement, and misuse of public funds. For instance, the United Kingdom's Bribery Act 2010, with its emphasis on corporate criminal liability, provides a stark contrast to the US approach, which often focuses more narrowly on individual actions. A comparative study reveals different levels of success in prosecuting high-profile individuals for abuse of power, highlighting variations in prosecutorial independence, witness protection programs, and the influence of political pressures. The UK experience, for example, demonstrates the complexities of investigating and prosecuting powerful figures within a highly interconnected and potentially influenced political environment. The difficulty in obtaining impartial evidence and ensuring witness safety, factors that are universally challenging in these types of cases, are compounded by the powerful individuals' ability to leverage their influence to impede the legal process.

Financial impropriety, another recurring theme in high-profile political scandals globally, offers further grounds for comparison. International anti-money laundering (AML) and combating the financing of terrorism (CFT) regulations provide a baseline against which to assess the President's alleged financial dealings. The Financial Action Task Force (FATF), an intergovernmental organization dedicated to combating money laundering, sets international standards that many countries have incorporated into their domestic laws. Compliance with these standards, however, varies widely, reflecting differences in enforcement capabilities, political will, and the overall level of corruption within a given jurisdiction. Analyzing how other countries have addressed similar cases of alleged financial irregularities involving high-ranking officials provides a benchmark against which to evaluate the investigative and prosecutorial responses in the President's case.

Cases from jurisdictions with strong AML/CFT frameworks, like those in Scandinavia or certain parts of Western Europe, provide valuable insights into effective strategies for uncovering and prosecuting complex financial crimes, even those involving sophisticated offshore accounts and shell corporations. The differences in legal approaches, prosecutorial resources, and judicial independence across these jurisdictions illuminate the multifaceted nature of achieving accountability in financial crimes related to political power.

Conflicts of interest, a common accusation in political scandals worldwide, present another area for comparative analysis. While the specifics of conflict of interest laws vary across countries, the underlying principle of ensuring transparency and avoiding the appearance of impropriety remains consistent. Some nations have stricter regulations than others regarding disclosure of assets, financial dealings, and relationships that could potentially influence official decision-making. Examining how other countries have addressed alleged conflicts of interest involving their leaders allows for an assessment of different approaches to regulation and enforcement. A comparative study might reveal the effectiveness of various mechanisms such as independent ethics commissions, stricter lobbying laws, and more robust asset disclosure requirements in preventing and addressing such conflicts. The experience of countries like Canada, known for its relatively strong ethics framework, provides a valuable case study for analyzing how institutional reforms can enhance accountability and public trust. Conversely, comparing this with countries where similar scandals have led to minimal consequences for those in power, showcases how weaker regulations and lack of enforcement can foster impunity.

The due process rights afforded to the accused also warrant international comparison. While the specifics of due process vary across jurisdictions, fundamental principles such as the presumption of innocence, the right to a fair trial, and the protection against self-incrimination are generally recognized under international human rights law. Analyzing how these rights have been applied in similar cases internationally provides a benchmark against which to evaluate the fairness and impartiality of the legal proceedings against the President. Comparative analysis might reveal variations in the speed and efficiency of legal processes, access to legal representation, and the availability of remedies in the event of procedural irregularities. This analysis will assess whether the process, in the President's case, aligns with international standards and best practices for ensuring fair treatment within the legal framework.

Finally, the role of international cooperation in investigations and prosecutions of high-profile individuals is crucial. Many financial crimes, for instance, transcend national borders, requiring effective collaboration between different law enforcement agencies and judicial authorities. Examining successful examples of international cooperation in similar cases reveals the challenges and opportunities involved in sharing information, conducting joint investigations, and ensuring mutual legal assistance. The experience of international bodies such as Interpol and Eurojust provides valuable insights into effective mechanisms for transnational crime prosecution. Furthermore, exploring how international treaties and agreements, such as mutual legal assistance treaties, have facilitated cross-border investigations in similar cases, highlights the critical role of international cooperation in enhancing accountability in high-stakes political cases that often involve a web of complex, cross-border transactions.

In conclusion, a comprehensive comparative analysis of international legal standards and practices, focusing on abuse of power, financial impropriety, conflicts of interest, due process, and international cooperation, reveals both the common challenges and the range of approaches used globally to address allegations against powerful individuals. While the specifics of legal frameworks and procedures might differ, the underlying principles of accountability and justice remain universally applicable. By studying successful and less successful approaches in other jurisdictions, we can better understand the strengths and weaknesses of the current system in the President's case and identify potential improvements for future investigations. This comparative analysis, far from offering a simple judgment on the President's actions, aims to contribute to a more nuanced understanding of the intricacies involved in pursuing justice and accountability within a complex political and legal landscape, providing crucial lessons for safeguarding democratic systems and promoting the rule of law worldwide.

Cross Cultural Perspectives on Leadership and Accountability

The previous chapter highlighted the stark contrast between the legal processes surrounding the allegations against the President and those found in other established democracies. However, the differences extend beyond mere procedural variations. A deeper examination reveals profoundly different cultural perspectives on leadership, accountability, and the very definition of acceptable conduct in public office. Understanding these cross-cultural nuances is vital to grasping the full complexity of the situation and avoiding simplistic, ethnocentric interpretations.

Consider the concept of "face" prevalent in many East Asian cultures. Maintaining "face," or social prestige and honor, is paramount. This emphasis on reputation can significantly influence how accusations of misconduct are handled. While a public airing of grievances and a rigorous legal process might be considered essential for accountability in the West, in some East Asian contexts, preserving the leader's "face" – even at the expense of full transparency – might be prioritized to maintain social harmony and avoid disrupting established hierarchies. This isn't to suggest a lack of accountability; rather, the methods of achieving it and the definition of acceptable compromises differ dramatically. A leader might be privately reprimanded, subtly pressured to resign, or offered a less public form of redress, all aimed at preserving the social fabric. This contrasts sharply with the often-public and adversarial nature of legal proceedings in the United States. The expectation of a detailed, transparent, and potentially humiliating public trial, which is viewed as a cornerstone of justice in many Western societies, might be seen as deeply inappropriate and culturally insensitive in other contexts.

Furthermore, the interpretation of leadership itself differs across cultures. In some collectivist cultures, leadership is often viewed as a responsibility towards the community, emphasizing harmony, consensus-building, and the collective good. Mistakes made by a leader might be seen as reflecting on the entire community, prompting efforts towards reconciliation and rehabilitation rather than harsh punishment.

Conversely, in individualistic cultures, leadership is more often perceived as an achievement reflecting individual merit, and failings are viewed as individual shortcomings deserving of appropriate sanctions, often with a strong emphasis on individual responsibility. This fundamental difference in the perception of leadership directly influences the approach to accountability. A leader's failures might be viewed as a systemic issue requiring collective reform in collectivist cultures, whereas in individualistic societies the focus might remain squarely on the individual's culpability.

The concept of due process also takes on diverse interpretations. While Western legal systems emphasize procedural fairness and the presumption of innocence, some cultures might prioritize restorative justice, focusing on repairing harm and restoring relationships rather than strictly adhering to formal legal processes. This is not to suggest a lack of justice, but rather a different approach to achieving it. The emphasis might be on mediation, reconciliation, and community-based resolutions, rather than the adversarial proceedings characteristic of Western legal systems. Furthermore, the degree to which evidence is admissible, and the role of witnesses can vary significantly. What might be considered admissible and persuasive evidence in one jurisdiction could be dismissed as unreliable or hearsay in another, leading to different outcomes in seemingly similar cases.

Consider, for instance, the differing approaches to financial transparency. In many Western democracies, strict disclosure laws mandate public reporting of financial dealings by public officials. Violations of these laws often lead to significant legal and political consequences. However, in some developing countries or nations with weaker regulatory frameworks, such transparency might be significantly less developed or enforced, leading to a different standard of accountability regarding financial impropriety. This is not necessarily indicative of corruption, but rather a reflection of differing institutional capacity and cultural norms. The absence of rigorous financial reporting, while problematic from a transparency perspective, shouldn't automatically be equated to intentional wrongdoing. The context of these practices requires careful consideration.

International cooperation in investigating allegations against powerful individuals also presents a complex landscape. The legal frameworks governing cross-border investigations and the willingness of nations to cooperate can vary widely, influenced by political relations, legal systems, and domestic sensitivities. While some nations maintain robust mechanisms for extraditing individuals or providing mutual legal assistance, others may be reluctant to cooperate due to political considerations or concerns about national sovereignty. This can significantly impede investigations spanning multiple jurisdictions, potentially hampering the pursuit of justice. For instance, some nations might be hesitant to share sensitive financial information due to privacy concerns or bank secrecy laws, effectively creating obstacles for investigators seeking a complete picture.

Moreover, the role of the media in holding leaders accountable differs dramatically across cultures. In some nations, a robust and independent press actively investigates and exposes wrongdoing, acting as a vital check on power. In other nations, state control over the media or the prevalence of self-censorship significantly limits the media's ability to scrutinize powerful figures, creating an information vacuum that hinders public understanding and accountability. This disparity in media freedom directly impacts the level of transparency and public discourse surrounding allegations of misconduct.

The President's case, therefore, cannot be analyzed solely through the lens of American legal standards and practices. A nuanced understanding requires acknowledging the broader global context, recognizing the profound cultural differences in perceptions of leadership, accountability, due process, and the role of institutions in safeguarding democratic norms. By considering these cross-cultural perspectives, we can avoid simplistic judgments and develop a more comprehensive and insightful analysis of the issues at stake, fostering a more informed and constructive debate about the future of accountability for leaders in the modern era. This comprehensive approach highlights the complexities involved and underscores the need for a comparative, culturally sensitive analysis to truly understand the ramifications of the allegations and their implications for the integrity of democratic governance, both domestically and internationally. Ignoring these cross-cultural dimensions would render any analysis incomplete and potentially misleading, thus hindering efforts to establish universally applicable standards for ethical leadership and robust systems of accountability. The challenge lies not merely in identifying instances of wrongdoing but in understanding the deeply ingrained cultural factors that shape perceptions of right and wrong, and in developing strategies for promoting ethical leadership and accountability across diverse societies.

Comparative Analysis of Legal Systems

To fully appreciate the complexities surrounding the allegations against the President, a comparative analysis of legal systems is crucial. The American system, with its adversarial nature and emphasis on individual rights, contrasts sharply with others. Consider, for example, the inquisitorial systems prevalent in many European countries. These systems, characterized by a more active role for the judge in investigating and gathering evidence, often lead to different outcomes and perceptions of fairness. In an inquisitorial system, the judge takes a more central role in directing the investigation and determining the truth, whereas the American system relies heavily on the opposing parties to present their cases. This fundamental difference can significantly impact how allegations of wrongdoing are handled and perceived. The President's case, viewed through this lens, reveals a system where the burden of proof rests heavily on the prosecution, a stark contrast to some systems where the onus of proving innocence might fall on the accused. This difference profoundly shapes public perception and the very definition of "due process."

The variations extend beyond procedural matters. Cultural attitudes towards leadership and accountability differ dramatically across nations. In some cultures, deference to authority figures is deeply ingrained, potentially influencing how accusations against powerful individuals are handled and perceived. Public opinion may be less critical, or dissenting voices may be suppressed. In other societies, a robust culture of transparency and accountability is firmly established, leading to a greater emphasis on independent investigations and stricter consequences for misconduct. The American system, though characterized by its checks and balances, has shown instances where the power of the

Presidency can influence the investigative process. Comparing this to systems with stronger independent oversight bodies, like those found in Scandinavian countries, highlights the potential vulnerabilities within the American framework. The strength of institutional checks and balances, therefore, becomes a critical factor in the comparative analysis, influencing the effectiveness of accountability mechanisms.

Take, for instance, the handling of financial disclosures and conflicts of interest. Many countries have stricter regulations and more transparent processes for monitoring the finances of public officials. A comparative analysis would reveal varying levels of scrutiny, ranging from detailed asset declarations and regular audits to more opaque systems with limited public access to financial information. The President's case necessitates an examination of how his financial dealings have been scrutinized within the American system compared to the standards in nations with stricter regulations. This comparison can highlight potential loopholes or weaknesses in the American system that allow for a blurring of lines between private interests and public duty. Such an examination reveals inconsistencies in the application of the law and raises questions about the effectiveness of existing regulatory mechanisms.

The concept of "due process" itself varies across legal systems. While the American system emphasizes procedural fairness and protection against arbitrary actions by the state, other systems may prioritize different aspects of due process. For example, some systems place greater emphasis on achieving a just outcome, even if it means deviating from strictly defined procedural rules. This difference in prioritization can significantly impact how the fairness of the legal proceedings is assessed. The President's case underscores this divergence by showcasing the potential for political influence on the legal process, a scenario less prevalent in some legal systems with more robust institutional safeguards. The analysis here requires a thorough understanding of each system's specific definition of due process and how those definitions are operationalized in practice.

Moreover, the role of the media and public opinion in influencing legal proceedings differs considerably across jurisdictions. In some countries, the media plays a more active and sometimes even adversarial role in investigating and publicizing allegations of misconduct, placing pressure on authorities to act. In other countries, the media is more tightly controlled or self-censors, leading to a less influential role in shaping public discourse and the legal process. The American context, with its robust and often highly partisan media landscape, adds another layer of complexity to the President's case. A comparative analysis would reveal how the media's influence on public perception and, subsequently, on legal proceedings varies significantly, depending on the legal and political culture of each nation. This variation impacts the pressure on institutions to act, affecting the timeline and the outcome of any investigation.

Furthermore, the availability of remedies and avenues for redress following a legal judgment also varies across legal systems. Some systems offer more comprehensive mechanisms for victims to seek compensation or other forms of redress, while others offer limited recourse. This difference in the availability of remedies highlights the unequal distribution of justice across legal frameworks. In analyzing the President's case, this aspect requires careful consideration of the legal and political possibilities for victims to obtain appropriate redress. The comparative approach reveals how the strength of institutions and the societal commitment to justice profoundly affect the effectiveness of the legal system in securing justice for those harmed by wrongdoing.

The varying approaches to criminal investigations, prosecutorial independence, and judicial review also warrant careful consideration. The level of independence enjoyed by prosecuting authorities and the power of judicial review mechanisms differ significantly across different legal systems. Some countries have more robust mechanisms for ensuring the impartiality of prosecutors and for challenging government actions through judicial review, while others may lack such safeguards. Analyzing the President's case through this comparative lens reveals potential weaknesses in the American system's capacity to ensure impartial investigations and independent judicial oversight, particularly when powerful individuals are involved. The examination of these variations allows for a critical evaluation of the effectiveness of legal mechanisms in ensuring accountability for high-ranking officials.

In conclusion, a thorough comparative analysis of legal systems is indispensable for understanding the complexities surrounding the allegations against the President. By examining the procedural differences, cultural attitudes, and institutional variations across different jurisdictions, a more nuanced and informed assessment can be developed, transcending simplistic, ethnocentric interpretations. This approach enhances the objectivity of the analysis and reveals the profound impact that the choice of legal and political framework has on determining accountability for those in power. The differences highlighted underscore the need for a global dialogue on best practices in ensuring accountability for leaders within a democratic framework, aiming to establish universally applicable standards for ethical leadership and robust systems of accountability across diverse societies. Only through such a comprehensive, comparative approach can we hope to foster a more informed and constructive debate about the future of accountability in the modern era.

Lessons Learned from International Precedents

Building upon the previous chapter's comparative analysis of legal systems, we now delve into specific international precedents to illuminate the complexities surrounding the allegations against the President. Examining cases with analogous circumstances in different jurisdictions offers a valuable lens through which to evaluate the American approach to such accusations. These comparisons are not meant to suggest direct equivalence—legal systems are deeply rooted in their respective cultural and historical contexts—but rather to highlight common threads and contrasting methodologies in handling allegations of high-level misconduct.

One crucial area for comparison involves the handling of financial irregularities by individuals in positions of power. Consider the cases involving prominent political figures in several European nations. In certain countries, investigations into alleged financial improprieties often begin with a thorough preliminary inquiry conducted by specialized investigative units, independent of the executive branch. These inquiries might involve extensive scrutiny of financial records, witness interviews, and potentially, the use of wiretaps or other surveillance techniques, all under the purview of judicial oversight. This contrasts sharply with the

American system, where the initial phases of investigation are often more decentralized and less judicially controlled, reliant heavily on investigative journalism and subsequent actions by law enforcement agencies, subject to political considerations. The different approaches to initiating investigations have profound implications for the speed and thoroughness of the process, as well as the perception of impartiality. In some European systems, once sufficient evidence is gathered, the case moves to a formal judicial inquiry that resembles the American grand jury system, but with greater judicial control. The emphasis is placed on uncovering the truth, with a less adversarial approach and often a greater role for the judge in directing the investigation.

Another key difference lies in the handling of conflicts of interest. Many nations have implemented strict regulations regarding the financial disclosures of public officials, coupled with robust enforcement mechanisms. These include independent ethics committees or commissions with the power to investigate potential conflicts of interest and impose sanctions, ranging from fines to removal from office. The strength of these regulatory frameworks and the independence of the enforcement bodies vary considerably across nations. In some countries, these bodies are largely independent of the executive, ensuring a more impartial process, whereas in others, the degree of political influence can impact their effectiveness. The American system, while possessing regulations on conflict of interest, arguably lacks the same degree of stringent enforcement and independent oversight found in certain international counterparts, leading to ongoing debates about the efficacy of existing mechanisms. Comparing the President's case to similar situations in countries with stronger institutional mechanisms reveals the potential strengths and weaknesses of the various approaches.

Furthermore, the concept of prosecutorial discretion, central to the American legal system, presents a vital area of comparative analysis. In many other jurisdictions, the decision to prosecute is less discretionary, with a higher threshold for initiating criminal proceedings. This often leads to fewer cases being brought to trial, but possibly with a higher conviction rate once proceedings commence. The American system, however, allows prosecutors considerable latitude in deciding whether to charge a crime, a decision influenced by a variety of factors including political considerations, the availability of resources, and the strength of the evidence. This discretionary power can lead to criticism, with allegations that it may be influenced by political motivations. Examining international precedents highlights the trade-offs inherent in this model, including the potential for unequal application of justice, and the need for enhanced transparency and accountability in prosecutorial decision-making. Cases involving similar allegations in other countries where prosecutorial discretion is more limited provide a valuable counterpoint, illustrating alternative approaches that may promote greater fairness and reduce the perception of political influence.

Beyond the purely legal aspects, the role of media and public opinion also differs significantly across jurisdictions. In some countries, the media landscape is more heavily regulated, with stricter limitations on investigative journalism and the reporting of ongoing investigations. This can limit public scrutiny of government officials but also minimizes the potential for prejudicing a case before trial. The American system, with its tradition of a free press and robust investigative journalism, exposes the potential benefits and drawbacks of unrestricted reporting. While a free press can be instrumental in uncovering wrongdoing and holding the powerful accountable, it also creates risks of biased reporting, dissemination of misinformation, and trial by media. Comparing the media coverage of the President's case to similar situations in countries with differing media landscapes reveals how the interplay between the press, the judiciary, and public opinion can significantly influence the trajectory and outcome of such investigations.

The handling of witness testimony also presents important contrasts. In some countries, witness protection programs are more robust and comprehensive, ensuring greater safety and encouraging cooperation with investigators. This is especially critical in cases involving high-profile individuals where threats or intimidation are a real possibility. Conversely, the American system, while possessing witness protection programs, has faced criticisms about their effectiveness and resources. A comparative analysis of how witness testimony was handled in comparable cases abroad provides insights into the challenges of securing truthful accounts and protecting witnesses, especially when dealing with powerful individuals. Learning from international best practices in protecting witnesses and ensuring the integrity of their testimony is crucial in striving for fair and just outcomes.

Finally, the concept of "due process" itself varies considerably across legal systems. The American emphasis on individual rights and the presumption of innocence is not universally shared. In some jurisdictions, the investigative process focuses more on establishing the truth, potentially at the expense of individual rights. By comparing the procedures employed in the President's case to comparable investigations in different jurisdictions, we can gain a deeper understanding of the strengths and weaknesses of the American approach to ensuring a fair trial, and the various ways other countries balance individual rights with the pursuit of justice. This comparative perspective illuminates not just procedural differences but underlying philosophical divergences regarding the balance between individual liberty and the collective interest in holding powerful individuals accountable.

In conclusion, while direct parallels between legal systems are impossible, the study of international precedents offers crucial insights into the handling of allegations against prominent political figures. Examining cases from diverse jurisdictions illuminates the strengths and weaknesses of different approaches to investigation, prosecution, and the protection of witnesses. By acknowledging both the similarities and the stark differences, we develop a more nuanced understanding of the complexities inherent in such high-stakes investigations, enhancing our critical analysis of the allegations against the President and fostering a more informed discussion about improving systems of accountability for public officials in the future. The lessons learned from these international parallels transcend the specifics of any one case; they offer valuable perspectives that contribute to a deeper, more comprehensive understanding of the broader issues surrounding justice, power, and accountability within the democratic framework. These comparisons are not meant to prescribe solutions but instead to enrich our understanding of the multifaceted challenge of holding those in power accountable in a just and equitable manner.

Summary of Findings and Key Arguments

Chapter Six

This book has undertaken a meticulous examination of the allegations of criminal activity leveled against a future President of the United States, juxtaposing them against claims of significant positive contributions to the nation. The investigation has spanned numerous avenues, delving into legal documents, scrutinizing media reports, and incorporating the analyses of legal experts from diverse backgrounds. Our primary focus has been on determining whether the actions attributed to the President meet the stringent requirements for criminal offenses under US law, and whether, at every stage, the principles of due process have been rigorously adhered to.

The journey through the preceding chapters has revealed a complex interplay of legal intricacies, political maneuvering, and public perception. We began by chronologically documenting the accusations, categorizing them into distinct legal frameworks, and observing the initial public reactions and the often-polarized media coverage. This initial overview served as a foundation for the subsequent, in-depth analysis.

Chapter Two delved into the evidentiary heart of the matter. We systematically analyzed financial records, presenting and interpreting forensic accounting evidence, alongside expert testimonies. The credibility of witness accounts was carefully assessed, acknowledging potential biases and inconsistencies. Physical evidence, where available, was examined, along with its chain of custody, to ensure its admissibility and probative value. The chapter also highlighted the various legal challenges and procedural issues encountered during the investigation and legal proceedings.

Chapter Three provided a detailed account of the legal proceedings themselves. We meticulously tracked the investigative phases, noting key decisions and the overall timeline. The complexities of grand jury proceedings, including the evidence presented and any resulting indictments, were meticulously dissected. The trial procedures were analyzed, focusing on the legal strategies employed by both sides and examining the merits of their arguments. We also reviewed significant judicial decisions and rulings, including the rationale behind them and their implications for the case. Finally, the impact of any appeals and post-trial developments was assessed.

Chapter Four ventured into the political landscape surrounding the allegations. We analyzed the highly charged political climate and its effect on public opinion, examining how political polarization influenced the narrative surrounding the allegations. A significant portion of this chapter was dedicated to understanding the media's role in shaping public perception, including an assessment of potential bias and the impact of media framing on public discourse. To further ground the analysis, relevant public opinion polls and surveys were presented and interpreted, demonstrating the shifting public sentiment throughout the various stages of the process. The impact on the President's approval ratings and political standing was also quantified and analyzed. Finally, the chapter assessed the wider political ramifications of the allegations and their overall effect on the nation's political landscape.

Chapter Five broadened the scope of the investigation by comparing the President's case to similar instances involving high-profile political figures worldwide. We examined pertinent international legal standards and practices, comparing them to those of the United States. This comparative analysis allowed us to gain insights into cross-cultural perspectives on leadership and accountability. A nuanced exploration of different legal systems and their approaches to similar cases provided a wider contextual framework for understanding the legal intricacies of the President's situation. Finally, this chapter drew valuable lessons from international precedents, enriching our understanding of the broader implications of the case.

In essence, this book presents a comprehensive and nuanced investigation. It's not simply a recounting of events, but a deep dive into the intersection of law, politics, and public image. The narrative avoids simplistic conclusions, instead aiming to provide a balanced, fact-based account that allows readers to form their own well-informed conclusions. The book's strength lies in its commitment to presenting a meticulously researched and thoroughly documented narrative.

The evidence presented throughout the book reveals a complicated picture. While certain allegations might appear to fall short of establishing clear-cut criminal culpability, based purely on evidentiary standards, others present a stronger case, depending on the interpretation of the evidence and the application of relevant legal precedents. The ambiguity stems partly from the inherent challenges of prosecuting powerful individuals, particularly within a highly polarized political climate. The access to resources, the influence wielded, and the inherent difficulties in overcoming the presumption of innocence all play a significant role in shaping the trajectory of such investigations.

The analysis of public opinion, media coverage, and political consequences reveals a profound impact on the American political landscape. The allegations, regardless of their ultimate legal outcome, have significantly impacted the President's legitimacy and public trust in institutions. The divisiveness generated by the accusations has underscored the need for greater transparency and accountability in government. Furthermore, the intense scrutiny surrounding the case serves as a powerful example of the complex interplay between law, politics, and public perception in a democratic society. The differing interpretations of the evidence and the legal arguments highlight the ongoing debate regarding the definition of criminal intent and the standards of proof required in high-stakes legal battles.

The book also demonstrates the crucial role of the media in shaping public discourse. While some media outlets provided balanced and fact-based reporting, others leaned towards partisan narratives, exacerbating the political divisions and further complicating the public's understanding of the allegations. This highlights the critical need for journalistic integrity and responsible reporting, particularly in politically charged environments. The intense scrutiny applied to this case underscores the importance of robust legal processes, the rule of law, and the necessity of protecting the principles of due process in all circumstances.

Finally, the comparative analysis reveals that this case resonates with similar situations globally. The challenges of investigating powerful figures, the intricacies of navigating complex legal systems, and the profound impact of such allegations on public trust are not unique to the United States. By considering international parallels, the book offers broader context and highlights the need for continuous reflection on standards of accountability and transparency across different jurisdictions. The ongoing need for reform and improvements to address

issues highlighted by the case also points to future directions for research and further investigation.

In conclusion, the book's findings highlight the need for ongoing vigilance in upholding the rule of law, the importance of robust investigative processes, and the need for a more nuanced and informed public discourse around complex legal and political issues. While offering a thorough analysis of the specific case in question, this book also serves as a wider commentary on the dynamics of power, accountability, and the ongoing struggle to maintain a just and equitable society. The implications for the future of American politics and democratic institutions are far-reaching and require careful consideration. The case remains a cautionary tale, reminding us of the constant need for ethical leadership, transparent governance, and unwavering commitment to upholding the principles of justice. The remaining unanswered questions and the areas identified for further research underscore the fact that the investigation is not merely a chapter closed, but a continued conversation on accountability, transparency, and the enduring struggle for justice in the face of power.

Assessing the Presidents Legitimacy

The preceding chapters have detailed the various allegations of criminal activity against the President, meticulously examining the evidence presented, the legal processes involved, and the interpretations offered by legal experts across the political spectrum. We have dissected the complexities of the legal arguments, weighed the strengths and weaknesses of the prosecution and defense cases, and considered the broader political context within which these accusations unfolded. Now, we must synthesize these findings to assess the impact on the President's legitimacy, a concept far more nuanced than a simple guilty or not guilty verdict.

Legitimacy, in this context, encompasses more than just legal compliance. It refers to the public's perception of the President's right to hold office, their belief in the fairness and integrity of their election, and their confidence in their ability to govern effectively and ethically. This perception is profoundly shaped by the allegations leveled against the President, the manner in which they were handled, and the ultimate outcome of the legal proceedings (or lack thereof). Even in the absence of a formal conviction, lingering doubts and unanswered questions can significantly erode public trust and undermine the perceived legitimacy of the presidency.

The allegations themselves, irrespective of their legal merit, have undoubtedly impacted the President's standing. The sheer volume of accusations, even if some are ultimately dismissed, creates a cumulative effect, fostering an atmosphere of suspicion and uncertainty. The media's role in disseminating these allegations, both responsibly and irresponsibly, further complicates the picture. The constant cycle of news reports, analyses, and opinions creates a fog of information, making it difficult for the public to discern fact from fiction, and consequently, to form a reasoned judgment on the President's legitimacy.

The handling of the legal proceedings themselves is another crucial factor. Even if the President is legally exonerated, the perception of fairness and impartiality within the justice system is paramount. Were the investigations thorough and unbiased? Were all relevant witnesses and evidence considered? Was due process scrupulously followed at every stage? Any perception of bias, favoritism, or procedural irregularities, regardless of the final legal outcome, can significantly damage the President's legitimacy in the eyes of the public. This is especially true in a highly polarized political environment, where accusations and counter-accusations are often amplified and manipulated for partisan gain.

The President's response to the allegations also plays a significant role in shaping public perception. Transparency and cooperation with investigations are essential for maintaining public trust. Conversely, evasiveness, stonewalling, or attempts to discredit investigators can further fuel suspicion and undermine legitimacy. The President's rhetoric, public statements, and choice of advisors also contribute to the overall narrative, influencing public opinion and affecting their assessment of the President's character and fitness for office.

\

Furthermore, we must consider the long-term implications of these allegations. Even if the President manages to navigate the immediate crisis and maintain a semblance of public support, the shadow of these accusations may linger, impacting their ability to govern effectively. The constant scrutiny, the need for damage control, and the potential for future revelations can all drain political capital and hinder the President's agenda. The erosion of trust, even if gradual, can have far-reaching consequences, weakening the President's ability to build consensus, pass legislation, and maintain effective international relations.

It is also crucial to examine the implications for the future. This case serves as a crucial precedent, illuminating potential vulnerabilities within the legal and political systems. Do current laws and regulations adequately address the unique challenges posed by powerful figures accused of serious crimes? Are investigative processes sufficiently robust and impartial to ensure fair outcomes? Are there mechanisms in place to protect the integrity of the electoral process from undue influence or manipulation? These questions require careful consideration and may necessitate reforms to safeguard the legitimacy of future presidencies.

The analysis presented in this book highlights the complex interplay between law, politics, and public perception. The assessment of a President's legitimacy is not a simple matter of legal pronouncements; it's a dynamic process shaped by a multitude of factors, including the nature of the allegations, the fairness of the legal proceedings, the President's response, media coverage, and public opinion. While the legal aspects are undeniably important, they do not tell the entire story. The impact on public trust, the erosion of confidence in institutions, and the long-term consequences for the political landscape must all be considered in a comprehensive evaluation.

Ultimately, the question of the President's legitimacy is not one that can be answered definitively with a single verdict. It requires a careful and nuanced examination of all the available evidence, a considered judgment on the fairness of the processes involved, and a thoughtful assessment of the broader political context. The findings presented in this book offer a framework for understanding the complexities of this critical issue, empowering readers to form their own conclusions about the intersection of law, politics, and the enduring challenge of maintaining a just and legitimate presidency. The case stands as a powerful reminder of the constant vigilance required to uphold the principles of accountability, transparency, and the rule of law, vital ingredients in the preservation of a healthy and functioning democracy. The unanswered questions and ongoing debates underscore the need for continued research and open dialogue, ensuring that future generations are better equipped to navigate the treacherous waters of political power and public trust.

The ongoing scrutiny surrounding the President's past actions serves as a cautionary tale, a stark reminder of the inherent tensions between the pursuit of power, the maintenance of public trust, and the unwavering commitment to upholding the principles of justice and fair play. The book's analysis encourages a more critical and informed understanding of the delicate balance between the legal requirements for conviction, the societal expectation of ethical leadership, and the complexities of political reality. By providing a detailed account of the various allegations, legal processes, and their multifaceted implications, this book strives to contribute to a more robust and informed public discourse, ultimately bolstering the capacity of citizens to critically evaluate those entrusted with power and to demand greater accountability from their leaders. The enduring importance of this narrative lies not only in its immediate implications for the current President, but also in its potential to inform future discussions about ethical leadership, the integrity of political institutions, and the pursuit of justice in the face of power. The exploration of this complex case offers valuable insights that can help strengthen democratic systems, promote transparency, and uphold the fundamental principles of a fair and just society. The future of American democracy, and indeed, the health of democratic systems worldwide, relies upon a continued commitment to these ideals. The conversations started here are not only important for the present, but also for generations to come, ensuring that accountability and ethical governance remain paramount in the pursuit of a just and equitable society.

Implications for the Future of American Politics

The revelations and legal battles surrounding the President's past, meticulously detailed in the preceding chapters, cast a long shadow over the future of American politics. Their implications extend far beyond the immediate consequences for the individual involved, reaching into the very fabric of the electoral process and the broader question of accountability for those in power. The case serves as a potent case study, highlighting vulnerabilities within the system and raising critical questions about the balance between presidential power and the pursuit of justice.

One of the most significant ramifications is the erosion of public trust. Regardless of the final legal judgments, the sheer volume of allegations and the extensive media coverage have undoubtedly shaken public confidence in the integrity of the presidency. This erosion of trust is not merely a matter of opinion; it has tangible consequences. Citizen engagement in the political process can suffer, leading to apathy and disengagement, particularly among younger voters who may become cynical about the possibility of meaningful change. Furthermore, a diminished faith in the presidency can weaken the country's standing on the global stage, impacting international relations and diplomatic efforts.

The case also raises serious questions about electoral integrity. The allegations against the President, if substantiated, suggest a potential manipulation of the electoral system through questionable campaign finance practices or other illicit means. This undermines the fundamental principle of fair and free elections, a cornerstone of a healthy democracy. The investigation's findings, or even the perception of a lack of thorough investigation, could embolden future candidates to engage in similar behavior, creating a climate of distrust and cynicism that threatens the very legitimacy of the electoral process.

The issue of accountability is paramount. The lengthy legal battles and political maneuvering surrounding the President's case demonstrate the challenges in holding powerful individuals accountable, even in the face of credible accusations. The complexity of the legal system, combined with the political polarization of the nation, can create a climate where justice is delayed, or even denied, depending on the political climate and the resources available to those involved. This lack of swift and certain accountability sends a troubling message, suggesting that those in positions of power may be shielded from the consequences of their actions. This can foster a culture of impunity, where individuals believe they can operate outside the bounds of the law without fear of significant repercussions.

The President's case also highlights the limitations of existing laws and regulations. The gaps in campaign finance laws, for example, may have inadvertently allowed for activities that, while not technically illegal, arguably undermine the fairness and transparency of the electoral process. This necessitates a critical review and potential reform of relevant legislation to better address emerging challenges and prevent similar situations from arising in the future. Such reforms should strive for a balance between protecting free speech and ensuring fair elections, a delicate equilibrium that requires careful consideration and robust public

Beyond legal reforms, the President's case underscores the urgent need for greater media literacy and critical thinking skills among the electorate. The sheer volume of information, often contradictory and biased, available through various media outlets can make it difficult for citizens to discern fact from fiction. The ability to critically analyze information, identify sources of bias, and evaluate the credibility of claims is crucial for informed participation in a democracy. Educational initiatives focused on media literacy and critical thinking are vital to empowering citizens to make informed choices and hold their leaders accountable.

The impact extends beyond the immediate political landscape. The case has undoubtedly fueled further political polarization and division within the country. The sharply divided opinions on the President's guilt or innocence, combined with the partisan nature of the legal and media coverage, have deepened existing ideological chasms. Bridging these divisions and fostering a more civil and constructive public discourse will require a conscious effort from all stakeholders – politicians, media outlets, and citizens alike. Promoting dialogue and understanding, focusing on common ground rather than emphasizing differences, is crucial to healing the wounds inflicted by the protracted controversy.

Furthermore, the case has raised important questions about the role of the judiciary in a politically charged environment. The perceived influence of partisan politics on judicial appointments and decisions has become a point of considerable concern. Maintaining the independence and impartiality of the judiciary is essential to ensuring the rule of law and upholding the principles of justice. Strengthening safeguards against political interference in the judicial system is vital to preserving public trust in the integrity of the legal process.

Looking ahead, the long-term consequences of this case remain to be seen. However, its impact on American politics is undeniable. It has exposed vulnerabilities within the system, raised serious questions about accountability, and highlighted the need for significant reforms in both the legal and political spheres. The ongoing debate and the actions taken – or not taken – in response to this case will shape the future of American politics for years to come. Whether this serves as a catalyst for positive change, strengthening democratic institutions and enhancing public trust, or further exacerbates existing divisions remains a critical question for the nation. The path forward necessitates a commitment to transparency, accountability, and a renewed focus on the principles of fairness and justice that underpin a healthy democracy.

The legacy of this case will ultimately depend on the nation's response – its willingness to confront these challenges head-on and to emerge stronger and more unified. The future of American politics hinges on this critical juncture, a moment demanding introspection, reform, and a renewed commitment to the ideals upon which the nation was founded. Failure to address the fundamental issues raised by this case risks further eroding public trust, weakening democratic institutions, and ultimately jeopardizing the future of the American experiment.

Recommendations for Reform and Improvements

The case surrounding the President's past actions, while undeniably complex and deeply divisive, offers a unique opportunity for meaningful reform and improvement across multiple sectors of American society. Ignoring the lessons embedded within this protracted legal and political battle would be a grave disservice to the principles of justice and democratic accountability. Addressing these issues requires a multi-pronged approach, focusing on enhancing legal processes, strengthening ethical guidelines for public officials, and fostering a more informed and engaged citizenry.

One critical area demanding reform is the process of investigating and prosecuting high-profile individuals, particularly those holding significant political power. The current system, as evidenced by the President's case, can be perceived as susceptible to political influence and characterized by delays and inconsistencies that undermine public trust. To mitigate these concerns, several key changes are necessary. First, the establishment of an independent investigative body, insulated from political pressure and with broad investigative powers, would ensure impartiality and thoroughness in examining allegations of wrongdoing. This body should be comprised of individuals with impeccable legal credentials and a demonstrable commitment to upholding the rule of law, free from partisan affiliations or potential conflicts of interest. The composition of such a body should be subject to rigorous scrutiny and public vetting to ensure its legitimacy and credibility.

Secondly, stricter timelines for investigations and prosecutions should be implemented to prevent drawn-out legal battles that erode public confidence. While due process is paramount, undue delays can create an environment where justice is perceived as slow and inefficient, allowing for narratives of evasion and obfuscation to flourish. Imposing reasonable time limits on investigations, coupled with transparent reporting mechanisms, would enhance the perceived fairness and efficiency of the process. This should not compromise the thoroughness of the investigation but rather streamline procedures to ensure swift and effective justice.

Furthermore, the current system's reliance on witness testimony, often subject to memory lapses, biases, or even deliberate falsehoods, necessitates a re-evaluation of evidentiary standards. The increasing availability and sophistication of forensic evidence, such as digital records and financial transactions, should be leveraged more effectively to supplement or corroborate witness accounts. Investing in advanced forensic technologies and training for investigators is crucial to ensuring the integrity and reliability of evidence presented in high-stakes cases. This shift towards a more technologically advanced approach to evidence gathering could dramatically improve the accuracy and reliability of investigations.

The ethical conduct of public officials is another critical area needing immediate attention. Current ethics regulations, while existing, often prove insufficient in addressing the complexities of modern political landscapes and the potential for conflicts of interest. Strengthening these regulations to encompass broader aspects of financial disclosure, lobbying activities, and potential for undue influence would create a more transparent and

accountable environment for elected officials. Increased transparency in financial dealings, coupled with stricter penalties for violating ethics regulations, will act as a deterrent against future abuses of power. This could include enhancing independent oversight mechanisms that are empowered to investigate potential breaches of ethics and impose meaningful sanctions.

Beyond the legal and ethical aspects, fostering a more informed and engaged citizenry is crucial to ensuring accountability. The proliferation of misinformation and partisan narratives often obscures the complexities of legal and political processes, making it difficult for citizens to form informed opinions and engage in meaningful civic discourse. Improving media literacy education in schools and promoting fact-checking initiatives will equip citizens with the necessary critical thinking skills to navigate the complexities of information overload. This investment in media literacy will contribute to a more informed electorate that is less susceptible to misinformation campaigns and better equipped to demand accountability from elected officials.

Furthermore, strengthening the role of investigative journalism is crucial. Independent and rigorous investigative reporting plays a vital role in exposing wrongdoing and holding powerful individuals accountable. This requires protecting journalists from undue pressure, intimidation, or legal harassment. Legislation protecting journalistic sources and safeguarding the right to publish investigative reports without fear of reprisal is essential to ensuring a free press that acts as a critical watchdog for the public interest. A healthy and robust investigative journalism sector ensures accountability and transparency in all sectors of society.

Finally, addressing the broader issue of political polarization and the erosion of public trust in institutions requires a concerted effort to foster constructive dialogue and promote civic engagement. Encouraging respectful discourse across different political viewpoints, promoting opportunities for civic participation, and celebrating the democratic process can contribute to a more cohesive and resilient society. This involves creating platforms for dialogue that transcend partisan divides, fostering a climate of mutual understanding, and promoting a sense of shared citizenship. Investment in programs aimed at promoting civic education and encouraging participation in the democratic process are crucial to enhancing public trust and fostering a more informed and engaged citizenry.

The case examined in this book serves as a stark reminder of the fragility of democratic institutions and the constant vigilance required to protect them. It is not simply a matter of prosecuting individuals but of reforming systems and strengthening safeguards to prevent similar instances from occurring in the future. Implementing the recommendations outlined above – establishing an independent investigative body, tightening ethical guidelines, investing in forensic technologies, enhancing media literacy, protecting investigative journalism, and fostering constructive dialogue – will require a sustained commitment from all stakeholders. However, failure to act decisively and comprehensively risks further eroding public trust, deepening political divides, and jeopardizing the future of American democracy. The path forward demands a collective commitment to transparency, accountability, and a renewed focus on the principles of justice and fairness that underpin a healthy and functioning republic. The legacy of this case should not be one of division and cynicism but rather one of meaningful reform and a strengthened commitment to the ideals upon which the nation was founded. The opportunity for positive change is significant, but only with concerted and dedicated action can the nation truly learn from this critical episode in its history.

Remaining Unanswered Questions and Areas for Further Research

The meticulous examination of the President's past actions, as detailed in this book, has unveiled a complex tapestry of legal ambiguities, political maneuvering, and shifting public perceptions. While we have strived to present a comprehensive and balanced account, based on available evidence and legal precedent, several crucial questions remain unanswered, demanding further investigation and analysis. These unanswered questions are not merely academic exercises; they represent critical gaps in our understanding that could significantly impact future legal and political discourse.

One of the most pressing areas needing further exploration is the extent of potential witness tampering or obstruction of justice. While certain allegations have been investigated, the sheer volume of individuals involved, and the complexity of the financial transactions involved necessitate a more thorough and independent inquiry. The potential for a coordinated effort to suppress evidence, influence testimony, or otherwise impede the course of justice deserves dedicated scrutiny. Access to previously sealed documents or testimony, protected under claims of executive privilege or attorney-client confidentiality, could prove invaluable in shedding light on this critical aspect. The application of advanced forensic accounting techniques could also unearth hidden connections and transactions that may currently remain obscured. This requires not only legal maneuvering to overcome existing protections but also a willingness from relevant parties to cooperate fully with such investigations.

Furthermore, the role of foreign influence in the President's past dealings needs additional examination. The accusations of foreign entanglements and potential quid pro quo arrangements require detailed investigation, going beyond the currently available public information. Access to international banking records, communication logs, and potentially classified intelligence could provide critical evidence to determine the extent and nature of any foreign interference. Experts in international law and financial regulations should be consulted to evaluate the legality of any uncovered transactions under relevant international treaties and national laws. This could require collaborative efforts between national and international investigative bodies, potentially necessitating the involvement of international courts or arbitration panels. The potential for future repercussions, both domestically and internationally, necessitates a comprehensive understanding of this aspect.

Another critical area requiring further research is the adequacy and impartiality of the initial investigations. Concerns about political interference, resource limitations, and potentially biased investigative practices have been raised by various commentators and legal experts. An independent review of the investigative process itself is crucial to assess whether all relevant evidence was collected, whether appropriate investigative techniques were employed, and whether any undue influence or bias impacted the findings. This is not simply about questioning the conclusions of past investigations; it is about evaluating the integrity of the entire process and identifying potential systemic weaknesses. This review could potentially highlight areas for reform within law enforcement and regulatory agencies, ensuring greater accountability and transparency in future investigations. The review should include detailed

examination of personnel files, budgetary allocations, and communication records pertaining to the relevant investigations, as well as interviews with investigators, prosecutors, and witnesses involved.

Beyond the immediate legal aspects, the broader political context warrants further investigation. The impact of the President's actions on public trust and confidence in democratic institutions deserves in-depth analysis. Quantitative and qualitative methods should be employed to assess the erosion of public trust, its potential consequences for political participation and stability, and the effectiveness of various strategies to restore public faith in government. This would require studying opinion polls, examining media coverage, conducting focus groups, and analyzing the impact on voter turnout and political polarization. Understanding the long-term effects of these events on the political landscape is vital for developing effective strategies to mitigate future risks to democratic governance. This could involve the collaboration of political scientists, sociologists, and communication experts to create a robust analysis of the complex interactions between the public, media, and the political system.

The role of media reporting and public perception also requires careful consideration. The selective dissemination of information, the influence of partisan bias, and the impact of social media on shaping public opinion necessitate a critical examination. Analyzing media coverage across different outlets, comparing the framing of the narrative, and studying the influence of social media algorithms on the spread of information are crucial steps in understanding the role of media in shaping public discourse and potential biases. This could require collaboration with media scholars and communication researchers to develop robust methodologies for content analysis and social media analysis. Additionally, the impact of "fake news" and disinformation campaigns needs to be thoroughly evaluated, considering their potential impact on the formation of public opinion and the erosion of trust in factual reporting.

Finally, the legal and ethical implications for future presidential candidates and public officials deserve careful scrutiny. The President's case provides a critical case study for developing clearer guidelines on financial disclosures, conflict of interest rules, and ethical standards for those seeking or holding high public office. The establishment of stricter regulations and more robust enforcement mechanisms is crucial to prevent similar situations from occurring in the future. This could involve consulting with legal and ethics experts to propose reform proposals, comparing best practices in other democratic systems, and considering the potential impact of new regulations on individual rights and the political process. A thorough cost-benefit analysis is crucial, considering both the potential prevention of future misconduct and the potential impact on candidate recruitment and governance efficiency.

The unanswered questions outlined above highlight the necessity for a continuous, multi-faceted approach to investigating the complexities surrounding the President's past actions. It is not a matter of simply concluding the case but of ensuring that the lessons learned contribute to strengthening democratic institutions, improving the legal processes, and bolstering public trust. This requires a sustained commitment from researchers, investigative journalists, policymakers, and the public to ensure that the issues raised are not only addressed but ultimately contribute to a more just and equitable society. The path forward demands collaboration across disciplines, utilizing cutting-edge research methodologies and fostering a climate of transparency and accountability. The opportunity to learn from this episode, to use it as a catalyst for meaningful reform, should not be squandered. The future of American democracy depends upon our collective willingness to engage with these unanswered questions with both rigor and responsibility. The pursuit of truth, and the application of that truth to foster improvements in our systems of governance, is a continuous process, not a single event. The journey towards a more just and accountable society is one that demands ongoing vigilance, critical analysis, and a firm commitment to the ideals of transparency and fairness.